Donald Trump

Lessons We Can Learn From Donal Trump

(Donald Trump's Life Lessons & Secrets to Success)

Dexter Bowen

Published By **Regina Loviusher**

Dexter Bowen

All Rights Reserved

Donald Trump: Lessons We Can Learn From Donal Trump (Donald Trump's Life Lessons & Secrets to Success)

ISBN 978-1-77485-749-6

No part of this guidebook shall be reproduced in any form without permission in writing from the publisher except in the case of brief quotations embodied in critical articles or reviews.

Legal & Disclaimer

The information contained in this ebook is not designed to replace or take the place of any form of medicine or professional medical advice. The information in this ebook has been provided for educational & entertainment purposes only.

The information contained in this book has been compiled from sources deemed reliable, and it is accurate to the best of the Author's knowledge; however, the Author cannot guarantee its accuracy and validity and cannot be held liable for any errors or omissions. Changes are periodically made to this book. You must consult your doctor or get professional medical advice before using any of the suggested remedies, techniques, or information in this book.

Upon using the information contained in this book, you agree to hold harmless the Author from and against any damages, costs, and expenses, including any legal fees potentially resulting from the application of any of the information provided by this guide. This disclaimer applies to any damages or injury caused by the use and application, whether directly or indirectly, of any advice or information presented, whether for breach of contract, tort, negligence, personal injury, criminal intent, or under any other cause of action.

You agree to accept all risks of using the information presented inside this book. You need to consult a professional medical practitioner in order to ensure you are both able and healthy enough to participate in this program.

Table Of Contents

Chapter 1: "My Entire Life Revolves Around Winning. I'm Not Prone To Losing Often. I Almost Never Lose." _____ 1

Chapter 2: "I Strive To Be A Better Person By Learning From My Mistakes, But I Make Plans For The Future By Only Focusing Upon The Current. It's Where The Fun Starts." _____ 5

Chapter 3: "I'm Extremely Competitive. I Like To Set Goals For Myself. It's Possible That's Not Always A Positive Thing. It Can Cause A Lot Of Stress." _____ 9

Chapter 4: "Money Wasn't A Significant Motivator For Me, Other Than As An Excuse To The Score. The Most Fun Is In Playing In The Sport." _____ 13

Chapter 5: "One One Of The Major Issues Of The Present Is That Politics Is A Sham And Good People Aren't Allowed To Get Into Politics." _____ 17

Chapter 6: "Sometimes The Best Investment Opportunities Are Those You Do Not Make." _____ 21

Chapter 7: "Sometimes After Losing A Fight, You Can Find A Different Strategy To Take On The Enemy." _____ 25

Chapter 8: "If Your Interest Is "Balancing" Your Work With Pleasures, You Should Stop Trying To Achieve Balance. Instead, You Should Make Your Work Enjoyable."
_____ 29

Chapter 9: "What Is The Difference Between Winners And Losers Is How An Individual Reacts To Every New Twist In Destiny." _____ 33

Chapter 10: "A Small Leak Could Make A Vessel Sink." _____ 37

Chapter 11: Negatives Of Donald Trump 44

Chapter 12: How Did The Donald Trump Administration Fail The U.S. Citizens __ 103

Chapter 13: The Donald Trump's Demise Donald Trump_____ 113

Conclusion _____ 182

Chapter 1: "My Entire Life Revolves Around Winning. I'm Not Prone To Losing Often. I Almost Never Lose."

Donald John Trump was born on the 14th of June 1946 at Queens, New York. He was the son of Frederick C. Trump was the father of two German immigrants who been settled in Bronx and was involved in real estate when he was 22 years before the time of Donald's birth. Frederick as well as his mom, Elizabeth Christ Trump, were the founders of Elizabeth Trump & son in 1923 (a business that later be renamed The Trump Organization) and the family was in an excellent economic position.

Donald was already a confident man in his early years, and his energetic personality led his parents to believe in his school, the New York Military Academy with his education because they believed that it would help define his character. his excellent performance allowed him to gain admission to Fordham University and, later in the

Wharton School of Finance at the University of Pennsylvania.

At Wharton He earned an education in Economics that is an excellent instrument for anyone who wishes to get into the world of business however this isn't the reason he became who is he today. It was his charismatic personality that has boosted his career. He was aware that he could get more money from the education was available to him, and had plenty of goals he hoped to realize when joining the family business that was eventually completely under his control in the year 1971. Since then, he's been able to make a number of profitable investment and luxury real estate developments, all while overcoming various challenges and being able to recover from bankruptcy.

If you are an entrepreneur, or even if you're looking to expand your business that you work for in, you must be in a position to stand apart. There will come a time that you have convince people to believe in you, show that you are knowledgeable about how to do it and convince the confidence of your potential customers. In this way, confidence can be crucial when you are trying to get an advertisement, or to attract an entirely new client or new investor.

Be prepared for these situations is essential to your business as the brilliant idea that prompted you to create it. While certain people, like Trump have a natural self-confidence but many lack the confidence to be able to achieve it. It doesn't require anything more than a little determination to see your confidence shine Dressing appropriately to important meetings is an excellent place to begin. This not only gives you an improved image and make it easier for us to be more authentic and feel secure both inside and outside. Being prepared to present what you are thinking about clearly, and think about related topics is more crucial. Be prepared to avoid surprises by formulating responses to questions or objections that might arise as well as avoiding to address subjects that you are not yet prepared to talk about.

What you must remember is the fact that trust is an integral part of what makes us earn confidence from others. Our honesty and integrity when doing business will show in the future however if we don't believe in our own abilities, we might not be able to reach that point. When you're trying to get to a higher professional level take a moment to be grateful for the achievements you've achieved thus far. Everyone hates someone who is always boasting about their accomplishments however there's nothing wrong in being honest in your work and showing the most positive aspect of yourself while conducting business.

Chapter 2: "I Strive To Be A Better Person By Learning From My Mistakes, But I Make Plans For The Future By Only Focusing Upon The Current. It's Where The Fun Starts."

On his Twitter page Trump attempted to emphasize that he's never bankruptcy-free and, in a sense, this is indeed the case. The casino business of Trump has applied for bankruptcy four times so far.

The collapse of Trump Taj Mahal in 1991 was the first and, if not the last, of all for Donald Trump. As per Clare O'Connor, journalist at Forbes magazine, "he did take a personal hit first time around. He had financed his construction project of Trump Taj Mahal with junk bonds, and was unable to pay the interest rate of a high. The business was in the negative, and so was he in the amount of $900 million of personal debt. In the mid-90s, he had reduced the majority of his debt by disposing of the Trump Princess yacht, his Trump Shuttle airline, and his stake in a number of other companies. Most importantly the fact that he stopped guarantying loans with his own money."

In the aftermath of bankruptcies, there was no impact on his personal wealth. Trump certainly learned that lesson from the very first time. Like everything other aspect of our lives, are prone to mistakes just the same way they grow from the success. Every time we make an decision that doesn't produce the desired results We have the chance to look at the factors which led to the mistake and then decide on the kinds of beliefs and ideas that could be most effective in our endeavor and which ones won't be suitable for the future in the same manner.

Mindfulness, also known as awareness of the current condition of our bodies and surroundings, is an idea that has its roots in Buddhism and can benefit all people, Buddhist or not. In actuality, a number of major businesses like Google, Apple and Procter & Gamble have trained their employees in this idea for some time recently, and have observed the positive effects it has had on their productivity. The course, which is not compulsory and has a lengthy waiting list and a large number of evidence-based benefits. It widens the gap between our initial impulse and the reaction we display when confronted with circumstances, leading to more effective decision-making. It assists us in focusing on the present task, increase productivity, and reduces stress, allowing us to have greater control over our emotions.

The greatest benefit is that you don't need to take a class to master mindfulness. It's all about clearing your mind of potential future outcomes , and instead focusing on working at the best possible level at the present moment in which we work. Each decision is influenced by the data we have right now, and there's no way to predict the future. What we are able to be sure of is that we are doing the best job when developing a product, implementing an innovative process, or offering our services. This, whether in the long or short-term is what will make our business successful and profitable.

Chapter 3: "I'm Extremely Competitive. I Like To Set Goals For Myself. It's Possible That's Not Always A Positive Thing. It Can Cause A Lot Of Stress."

Donald Trump has always had an eminent showman's presenceone that he been able to display on his reality television show before he entered politics. In the form of anger, provocation, or just sheer the ability, depending on whom you talk to Trump managed to capture the attention of people even before his first appearance in a debate on the political scene. However, entering the political world isn't easy to even the best intelligent candidate, and it certainly took some time to prepare his to actually show up for the challenge.

Each challenge we face that we face, whether self-imposed or from the outside it is an opportunity for us to gain knowledge about the topic we are being challenged with, as well as concerning ourselves and our limits and the capabilities we have.

What we do and the things we don't do is important, as is everything we accomplish and each failure we make. If we've never put ourselves through the test (and thus have only a superficial understanding of what we could actually accomplish) How will we be able to establish goals for any growth?

The importance of goals is in their successbecause they set the course of action to follow and can be a great method of staying engaged. The purpose of making goals, be it for your own life or your business, is to achieve things you've never attempted to do and, as simple as it may sound, usually means doing things you've never done before. So, setting goals will likely force us outside of our comfort area and challenge us to go beyond the perception of our limits. That's where things could become a little tricky: You'll need to keep an objective view. If your idea isn't viable, it could frustrate and be negative. Engaging in challenging challenges in a progressive manner can be a great thing.

When it comes to managing the work of a team objectives are the main thing we must be aware of when planning strategies, reviewing results, and assigning people. The more specific and complete your goals are more straightforward it is to communicate the goals with others and ensure everyone is to the same place. Timing is an essential aspect of any good goal regardless of whether they're short-term or long-term it's crucial to establish a deadline you will reach at some point because it will increase the motivation to accomplish it.

In the business world, a short-term objective is one intended to be achieved in less than a year and a mid-term objective is one that is to be accomplished within three years from the time the goal is established, and an objective for the long term would encompass everything we would like our business to be able to accomplish within five years. The longer they go back it is, the less specific they are, and the reverse is also true. They are all equally significant as components of a bigger picture that could be smaller than a one individual entrepreneur or as large as a company that has hundreds of workers. While a large part of the fact is that bad planning could result in a virtually irreparable catastrophe but the other is that nothing can happen if you don't make a move and implement your plans. Sometimes, just a single step is enough to initiate an unintended chain reaction in which we are able to conquer other obstacles and dismantle the false notions of limits.

Chapter 4: "Money Wasn't A Significant Motivator For Me, Other Than As An Excuse To The Score. The Most Fun Is In Playing In The Sport."

There are those who believe that the only reason behind Donald Trump's success is that the family he came from was wealthy. It's not a fact that the family he was raised in enjoyed an upscale lifestyle before he even learned to walk, but to be honest, he was the one to make the choices that led to the Trump name famous beyond the world of business. Trump has turned the brand into a name that has been put on his casinos, but on an array of luxury products including steaks, wines and cologne, to clothing and furniture.

But, as he's said that it's the real estate market that has always motivated the way he conducts business: "It's tangible, it's sturdy, it's beautiful. It's artistic from my perspective and I enjoy property."

One of his first tasks when he was working for the Trump company, when it was owned by his father was the renovation of the apartment complex they were the owners of in Chicago. The outcome of the plan that he implemented included an increased occupancy rate of nearly 200% and a $6.75 million dollars deal after selling it within a short time.

His next major opportunity was with The Commodore Hotel located in New York, which he bought right at the time it was set to close and then transformed it into the extremely successful Grand Hyatt hotel in just four years. In the meantime the hotel was already a distinct entity him and his The (now changed name to) Trump Organization from the family-owned company which was not very well-known and which offered housing mostly for middle-class clients.

It is possible that you already know what you want to accomplish and just have to put it into practice, but if don't, try imagining you're part of the Trump family. Imagine that all your wants and desires are met as you consider what is something you would like to work on regardless of money? Make sure you are honest before you get to the "how can I earn money with it" aspect. In the end, being innovative is essential for success in business and there are a myriad of opportunities for everyone's interests. One excellent example is a small surf school located in Calgary, Canada. The owner is a personal trainer who enjoys surfing, took his passion and transformed it into a lucrative company , even in a city that is so far away from the ocean.

There's an article written by a career coach Chrissy Scivicque which argues the opposite. She eliminates Confucius famous quote "choose an occupation you enjoy and you'll never be required to spend a single day of your entire life." She says that our perception of the things that we like can change when they are turned into work. She believes that work isn't play, and she is completely true. But, we're all grown-ups and are aware of the way things work and we are aware that we need to rise every morning and accomplish something that will allow us to pay for our rent or mortgages, and also save for the trip we've always wanted so badly. It's real to point out that there'll be more pressures that weren't present as long as we kept the hobby a passion However, we shouldn't forget that the majority of our lives is spent at work and that it's a shame to not take pleasure in the process. It's a lot of work and effort, just as love. Could a little hardship be enough motivation to leave an unsatisfying life?

Chapter 5: "One One Of The Major Issues Of The Present Is That Politics Is A Sham And Good People Aren't Allowed To Get Into Politics."

Being elected president of the United States, to make decisions that impact over 318 million Americans and affect many foreign countries, will alter the course of a person's life. However, even earlier in the election in between the debates and other public appearances the impression of the Trump brand has changed completely. The public would view him as a successful mogul of real estate, however nowadays, many see him as a symbol of ideas they'd like to see implemented throughout the country.

In a new analysis of the rise of Donald Trump into the political arena, M. Haberman and A. Burns -- each of them journalists for The New York Times -- declare that running for president was about earning respect. "Repeatedly dismissed as an uninvolved court jester or a silly showman the Trump was a shrewd and savvy politician. Trump muscled his way into the Republican elite with the help of will...At every turn, the those in the Republican establishment hoped that they could side to Trump. Trump just enough to keep him from being quiet or to get him out of the way. However, what the party's leaders saw as a kind gesture or ego-stroking of the Mr. Trump -- speaking in public at events, meeting with candidates in the pipeline, appearances with Republican bigwigs were used to increase his standing and eventually establish himself as a dominant persona for the 2016 election."

Respect for the common good between citizens and the representatives of their respective parties is the basis of politics upon, not power or money. However, unfortunately the way Trump declares is correct People with best intentions, the right people, aren't likely to engage in it.

It does not have to be like this. Even even if you're not an active political person, being involved in your community , whether as a business or personally could bring enormous advantages. Apart from the social networking and brand recognition through community involvement it is also possible to create positive changes in your town or community that could bring benefits to both you and your family.

It could be sponsoring a local youth team or joining the Chamber of Commerce, people would like doing business with companies who care about the community who surround them.

If you're unhappy with a regulation or decision made by your council make sure you bring it up at the city hall in the public session. Or, you can contact your council members to address your concerns. Make sure you identify yourself as the owner or a member of your company to boost your credibility.

Find local teams in sports and farmers' markets, or other events that you can be a sponsor or volunteer for in exchange for the opportunity to display your name on the site such as, for instance, or to display banners at the event or of their team jerseys. You might want to consider hosting an event on your own, and then contact others local companies to find out whether they'd like to be involvedtoo.

If you're somewhat political and think that you could be a changemaker and you are able to make a difference yourself, think about running for office. Even if you do not win like Trump has demonstrated that he can, it's an excellent opportunity to build brand recognition and exposure for your business.

Chapter 6: "Sometimes The Best Investment Opportunities Are Those You Do Not Make."

Being successful in the field of business requires determination. Going beyond your personal limits and taking on the risk each investment is part of the equation. It's also a an aspect of learning which requires a certain amount of prudence to evaluate situations and decide what is the most appropriate time to make the investment of time and money and when it's time to walk away.

From a financial standpoint from a financial perspective, a business and an individual aren't the same. Everyone owns assets (such as clothes, a car houses, etc.).) and liabilities (loans and cardholders,, and other charges to pay) similar to for a business the difference in favour of liabilities results in bankruptcy. Both types of investments can be made in order to boost their wealth and achieve different goals, but the funds invested can only be considered an asset if you make good decisions. If they do not then it will instantly add to their financial obligations.

Investments that are not sound could cause more damage than inactivity, as they can eat the negative balance of our accounts and could lead to an economic crisis. Some investments aren't excellent and not all can be easily recovered from. There is an array of questions to ask ourselves prior to letting our curiosity and enthusiasm become overwhelming:

Is this fund fit my profile?

It's never a good choice to put your money into a company that you aren't sure about. Even if you offer capital, but not knowing the business is difficult to predict changes in the market if you're not certain what to consider. Your risk-aversion level is also that is crucial, as your VAR (Value at Risk) of any investment may be quite different. A higher VAR could depend on the anticipated return however, would you be in a position to cover the loss and reinvest in capital if there was a problem?

* Do I have to take out a loan?

The wrong investment decision with your assets will already affect your financial situation, but investing it using someone else's money could result in a disaster, because you'll be committing the risk of a debt you might not be able repay. Even in the most ideal scenario, there's an opportunity that interest could end in taking the majority (or almost all) of your profits.

* How much time and money have I put into forecasting the results?

There is a lot of research to complete prior to making any kind of investment. You must be aware of the risks, the costs and commissions, tax-related implications and more. It's best to consult with a professional before making any decision, but the advice they provide should be nothing more than an additional detail added to the research you have to conduct yourself.

Do my portfolios have diversification?

Diversifying your investments is the exact opposite of putting all your money into one asset. Through diversification of your portfolios,, you lower the risk and consequences of losses.

* Do I need to get the money in the near future?

Investments require the right amount of time to show results, meaning you'll have to wait until you can recover the money you invested and also to earn any earnings. So, do not invest in an investment without knowing the duration of time that the money you invest in it is compatible with your requirements and expectations.

There's always some uncertainties in investments, however the above questions can be a good first step to lessen it and gain an improved understanding of the things we're doing. Information, in the way that it is, is valuable.

Chapter 7: "Sometimes After Losing A Fight, You Can Find A Different Strategy To Take On The Enemy."

However, Donald Trump, being a experienced businessman who has been investing for decades, has faced certain financial difficulties similar to those discussed in chapter two of the book. The first was disastrous for him as the assets of his family were at risk. This was a huge lesson that prompted Trump to act differently in the future with his companies.

It's also important to note that this did not hinder him from doing his job.

Everyone hates to fail However, that it can happen to even the most successful people we could mention. It is best to look at it from a different angle and see it as an experienceand an opportunity to learn insights that will prove useful for the next time. A partner to discuss the situation with could make it more straightforward to identify what went wrong , and create a better plan to plan for future.

Regressions can undermine our faith or hinder our motivation in the event that we don't deal with each one at a time. As the author William Ward once said, "man as well as bridges, were made to bear the weight that is at hand, but not the weight of the entire year in one sitting."

Be prepared for every obstacle that it arises is much more enjoyable to deal with in the end rather than building up frustration and anxiety. The most important thing is to not forget to celebrate your successes as well. Reminding yourself of your successes can help you remember everything you are able to accomplish.

Maintaining a positive outlook is one of the most important aspects in helping your company recover from the aftermath of a crisis. If your attitude is in the right direction by implementing these tips will not only make life easier but also more beneficial:

- Take action to fix the problem. When you are in a the midst of a crisis, your entire situation can be shaken. You won't be at the same spot in the future when you're in a position to restore your normal flow of things. It is therefore essential to start by conducting an examination of your costs, incomes, debts as well as all other aspects that is related to your finances prior to making any decisions.

Rethink your goals. Since your circumstance has changed, you may find that your goals require a slight change. For instance, paying off some debts, as an instance, might be on first on the list to lower interest.

* Put the new plan into effect in the shortest time possible. There's no way to get through an emergency unless you're ready to act. A new strategy could be fantastic however it's unimportant until you implement it out. Therefore, regardless of how complex and static your situation may appear remain focused and avoid getting lost in your goals.

* Find another option to earn money. If you're an entrepreneur, you might come up with a method to offer an additional service for your clients, or if you're facing a financial crisis , you can get involved in a lucrative side-job (like selling your artwork, teaching your skills or a particular subject, etc.). However be sure to adhere to a set budget and do not spend too much.

Reorganizing your home is a laborious process It is possible that you will need to put in more effort than you did before for some duration. But, recovering from financial turmoil is feasible in most instances so long as you are determined, focused and committed.

Chapter 8: "If Your Interest Is "Balancing" Your Work With Pleasures, You Should Stop Trying To Achieve Balance. Instead, You Should Make Your Work Enjoyable."

If there's a particular memory which Donald Trump likes to bring to mind when discussing the past, it's the experience as host on an reality show that was the show of his choice for fourteen complete seasons. The Apprentice that broadcast in 2004, saw an average of 20.7 million viewers in its initial season. It has it has continued to be a major success on American television afterward. The show features entrepreneurs compete for an enormous amount of money and a deal to join the massive Trump Organization.

"I enjoyed incredible success in show business as a celebrity in the Hollywood Walk of Fame. The Apprentice was among the most popular shows," he said to Time Magazine in one of his many memories of the show. For someone who has spent to a career that has turned his brand into a household name with a TV show, an appearance at the Walk of Fame are definitely impressive accomplishments. Trump has the respect of the media, and with The Apprentice he matched that enthusiasm for fame with his experience in business.

If you're in a position to work for yourself or trying to find it, establishing a job project that actually brings together your interests could be much easier than while working for an employer. A few suggestions on how to determine the best direction for doing something that is motivating you are covered at the end of which focuses specifically on business concepts which are still in the design stage. However, attaining a greater satisfaction from the space you have already set is a choice you are able to take, regardless of whether the space is yours to own or not.

In rare instances, work can be demanding. We are subject to a set of deadlines, rules and obligations we must to fulfill which could be stressful if managed properly. And stress from day to day, like we all do is an emotional drain that leaves very little time to enjoy our work. Thus it is a simple task of altering the way we manage our work can provide massive relief, an initial step toward having a more enjoyable working week. Make a list of tasks for every day, listing priority items on top, and creating a separate section for tasks that can wait, but are perfect to fill in any gaps of free time. It is also possible to install one of the numerous personal assistant programs available that are available, many of which are available for free and completely customizable to meet your requirements. As much as you'd like to finish your entire week in the first two days, try to be realistic of the amount of time you'll need for each job and the amount of time you'll require to stretch your legs, get some coffee and keep your head on straight.

These little breaks are essential. Google, NASA and a numerous other important companies already know this, and they encourage employees to take short but regular breaks to increase their productivity. If you can be productive and accomplish your goals you planned for the day, chances that you won't need to work from home or cut back on the time you spend on your weekends to complete all the work that was not completed in the week. The main reason we work so hard is to invest our earnings in things that matter to us. A great meal together with family, an weekend getaway or another of the numerous things which keep us motivated and relaxed.

Our personal lives help us see work from a different the context of our lives. No matter what the importance of our work or how much time it requires from our schedule It's not the only thing that makes us who we are. Be mindful of this during times of difficulties at work is essential if we want to keep a healthy balanced work-life balance.

Chapter 9: "What Is The Difference Between Winners And Losers Is How An Individual Reacts To Every New Twist In Destiny."

One of the reasons many people think of Trump as an effective leader not that he has not failed in business (which we've read in the previous chapters, isn't factual) instead, because of his approach to dealing with his failings. Every leader must be ready to take matters in their own hands and steer the team in the most effective direction whenever things go wrong. Any leader can get the ire of team members and subordinates if they are unable to manage the circumstance.

In the first place, the leader must show dedication to the mission and its accomplishment. They should be dedicated to their colleagues, to work as a team instead of trying to carry out individual tasks that may not perform as effectively as a team work. Leaders strive to help others realize their full potential. They update the team of their progress and provide them with every update regarding the situation as frequently as they can, sometimes even via one email per day. They make sure to go over all the important steps at staff meetings, and to ensure that everyone has the opportunity to ask questions and understand the procedure fully. This is an essential aspect of the professional mindset and the desire to achieve excellence in your own life. There's always a quicker way, or shortcut, and it's quite possible that nobody will have any major concerns with a task that was done properly and on time. But, aiming for the best possible outcome is a hallmark of a professional approach.

This is the image that you must portray to keep employees involved in the company at ease and focused in the face of the possibility of a crisis. It is not necessary to dismiss all worries or pretend that there's nothing to worry about in the situation, which could have a negative impact on all employees. Resilience is essential for leadership positions, not only as a characteristic but also to set an example for others which is why overreacting and expressing negative emotions is best avoided.

An unresponsive leader could cause more problems and certainly won't aid in solving any problem. It's not uncommon to find some push their teams too hard to try and solve the problem, causing the team to feel exhausted and discouraged by the challenge of achieving every goal while at the same time. It is also common to see leaders who become somewhat dictatorial during crises because they believe that putting more pressure on their employees will improve the situation quickly, when it isn't the situation.

Learn more about how to deal with common business issues in the following chapter. If you are faced with an issue that is complex, right before you reach the resolution phase I'd like you to slow down and take a breath. The act of pause during an opportune moment could be the opposite of our initial reaction however it's the most effective thing to do. Be sure to take your time to analyze the situation and formulate an appropriate response. You need to make yourself believe that you have the ability to make the situation better before you attempt to convince others. First impressions matter and the trust of your team is something you should risk losing.

Chapter 10: "A Small Leak Could Make A Vessel Sink."

It takes some period of time for even a small leak to cause a vessel to sink I'll admit that. However, most startups are prone to multiple (not very obvious) leak. This will certainly accelerate the process. In addition, it's crucial to be aware how even the slightest crack may begin to expand when we choose to not pay attention to it. This is why it's crucial to keep recognizing the signs, to look for them and then work on them until they're no longer a danger.

The most difficult to identify are those that are caused by the inefficiencies of your team. The greater the number of individuals involved in your project, the more difficult it becomes to keep track of everything. If, like many new entrepreneurs, haven't been in control of everything that happens in your business It is possible to begin by paying attention to the specific aspects that affect the various areas, like:

* Time exploitation. It is true that time costs money they claim, and it's also one of our scarce resources. How employees spend their time must align with the objectives they're expected to achieve setting specific priorities will benefit your team greatly.

* Resource exploitation. Inefficient utilization of any of the resources used by the company is not only unsustainable but also results in economic losses that could increase at the end of every month. The process of educating your employees about responsible consumption won't take any time, but will pay dividends in the short-term.

- Procedures and systems that are implemented. If you're in charge of the project, it is your responsibility since you , along with any other team members who you have may be the ones that must decide how things must be conducted to ensure the standard you're hoping for. Learn about each individual's abilities, background and requirements prior to establishing schedules or assigning tasks or resources. Each employee is not qualified for the same role.

Regarding this final point There could be problems with the plans that are in use regarding marketing your brand. Have you conducted any research about the image your business is presenting to the general public? What was the response you received from your previous marketing campaign? Today, social media is a fantastic method to obtain the answer for these queries directly from the intended public and a review of these responses will assist you in correcting their impressions in the event of a need.

It is also a great tool in finding out how much satisfaction that customers currently have when they trust you and learning about their needs or suggestions to help offer something more effective and determining whether you've managed to create an emotional bond with your customers. There are many companies that utilize professional software to record all public posts that reference their brand or product and organize them according to certain parameters of information to produce excellent marketing research. You can however, see plenty of this by signing your company to the most popular social media and actively participating in conversations with the general public. This, in addition to being a desirable side effect, can also allow you to build relationships and build their trust.

After having thoroughly reviewed all of this information and discovered the leaks, you'll be required to develop the best way to prevent them from happening. It may be difficult initially, particularly when you realize that there are many issues that require attention (and which contribute to the issues that you need to be attending to) however, it's very achievable if you take the proper steps:

Sort them into order. Most likely, each issue will fall in a distinct category:

Non-urgent, low impact issues that you can't tackle at all Follow up later to ensure they do not get worse.

The most urgent issues are those with low impact that need to be addressed in a manner that does not require a huge amount of physical or human resources.

Important non-urgent issues that have high impact, that require a thorough planning of short and long-term goals.

Important, urgent issues that are, of course your main concern and may require the creation of a dedicated team to take on these issues full-time.

Be open about your capability to solve these problems. There are certain issues, like complex financial issues, that may require the assistance by an expert (for example accounting professionals). Do not try to repair something that you and your partner don't have the expertise to handle, especially when it's a major issue.

* Plan your strategy. After the priorities are set and you know whether other parties are helping to solve the problem it is essential to create a comprehensive plan (the more

complicated the issue is and the more detailed the strategy) with precise due dates. This is not an easy task that can be done by one person therefore it's ideal to collaborate with the entire team who have responsibility for the affected areas.

• Get your team members involved. The plan must be detailed with a reason and this is due to the fact that it is essential to explain it to the entire team. Set aside time to hold an appointment with your entire team to explain the situation and then present the game plan and the deadlines to all team members. Involving them in the process is a great method of involving them in the process of solving problems and is the only method to ensure that your strategy will work.

* Compare. Be sure to keep an eye on all the data you collect prior to and after implementing the changes you have made, as their comparability will tell you whether your decisions are in the right direction or if you require an additional adjustment.

The right procedure is what has helped keep this Trump Organization afloat even when the worst-case scenario was averted. This, however, is the result of many years of experience, and most of all, a solid group of advisors working to bring it about. Be sure to learn from your mistakes and surround yourself with the most qualified people, and possess the ability to critically and challenge yourself. Then, you too will discover the path to success.

Chapter 11: Negatives Of Donald Trump

Methods by which are the ways that Trump administration has affected Americans.

Economy

The lodging installments for homebuyers who are new by around $500 in the year 2017. The day it was announced that it was in effect, the Trump group switched over to an Obama group's operation to reduce Federal Housing Administration, or FHA charge for contract protection for homebuyers who are new by 25 premise-focused focuses on the possibility of bringing down the monthly installments of home loans for 1 million families who are buying or refinancing their homes in the last year.

The Department of Labor has been criticized for its trustee rule that could have required retirement consultants to behave in the clients the best financial interest. President Trump has delayed the application of the standard by 60 days , and has asked the department to reconsider the rules. This could make it more difficult to put aside money to retire, since excessive charges from conflicted exhortations cause savers to lose an estimated $17 billion every year.

Court proceedings were delayed on the Obama organization's extra-time development, but did not protect the laborer's rule of thumb. This rule would have increased wages for workers by an average of $12 billion over the next decade and extended additional time guarantees to 4.2 million more Americans. In his confirmation hearings, Labor secretary candidate Alexander Acosta proposed he endeavor to eliminate the second time-based rule.

The delayed need for a standard to limit the exposure of laborers exposed to dangerous silica particles for about a quarter of one year. After more than 40 years of development the standard will protect workers in assembly and development against breathing silica dust, which causes cellular damage inside the lungs. It also causes silicosis persistent obstructive pulmonary sickness as well as kidney infection. It is expected to save around 600 life and prevent the emergence of more than 900 cases of silicosis each year.

The executive order was canceled. Fair Pay and Safe Workplaces Executive Order which ensured that contract workers and administrative employees adhered to specific assurance laws prior to signing government contracts. The demand was to require companies to cooperate in conjunction with authorities from the government in order to expose violations of the law and to be in compliance prior to accepting new contracts. A lot of workers will be vulnerable to wage theft or work-related wounds and segregation at work due to the decision to cancel. Also, the proposal could have protected women by preventing restricted mediation due to the aforementioned rape, bullying and separation cases.

The Trump administration has backed efforts in Congress to reduce government spending on the wealthy that to store in the Affordable Care Act, or ACA. As part of the Congress's efforts to repeal and replace the ACA and replace it with a new one, President Trump confirmed a plan that would have meant the 3.8 percent net personal expenditure would be revoked for $157 billion for a period of more than 10 years ago, as stated by the Congressional Budget Office, or CBO. The plan is to fund important projects that will meet human needs for daily comforts and security in retirement for many working Americans. In light of Trump's rent land payments by itself, The Wall Street Journal found that the cancellation would save Trump $3.2 million dollars in costs in 2016 .

Trump has tried to cut the government's expenditures by a lot of dollars while removing medical insurance from many Americans. Based on President Trump's release of in 2005 Tax Return Form 1040, repealing the ACA could grant Trump the tax cut worth more than $2 million. At the same time the House approval to end the ACA would have removed medical insurance from the hands of more than 24 million Americans.

He assembled the wealthiest financial industry leaders to encourage the change in duty that he was certain would benefit the working classes. This code of conduct is an instrument for deciding when exclusive privileges are granted to specific interests. In spite of his promise to cleanse the badlands the president Trump has assembled a group of elites to create his assessment reform plan

* Three former Goldman Sachs chiefs, Steve Mnuchin, Gary Cohn, and Steve Bannon

* Two other head of the business account, Justin Muzinich and Craig Phillips

* Prior duty lobbyist on behalf of Fidelity Investments, Shahira Knight

This made it harder for veterans to get jobs by imposing a recruitment freeze for the government. Veterans have a distinct attraction to government positions and 33% of the recently employed bureaucratic employees during 2015 had been veterans. No matter if a variety of jobs in VA, the Department of Veterans Affairs or VA are exempt from the freeze on hiring, the other vacant positions will, in all likelihood be unavailable at other government agencies.

It has proposed spending cuts that could decimate rural America. The spending plan of President Trump will eliminate projects that aid in the creation of rustic jobs, accommodation foundations, medical services as well as monetary turn events. If they are implemented the spending cuts will eliminate moderate space for many fighting rustic families; end jobs in network administration for 18,000 elderly residents in the country territories and also provide necessary support for carriers' associations, which serve 175 provincial and small networks.

It was suggested to significantly cut jobs preparing and workers' pay and welfare implementation. The President has suggested that the fiscal budget for 2018 could result in 2.7 million adults and teens being denied access to job preparing and business administrations in the year 2018.

They have suggested spending cuts that could cause clogging of the streets and reduce financial viability. The plan calls for eradicating off the TIGER award program of the U.S. Branch of Transportation, or USDOT that funds creative transportation projects on the surface. Additionally, the funding is contingent on the completion of New Starts program inside the Federal Transit Administration, which is a major public transportation project. Train and transport speedy transport projects reduce pollution of the air and street, and also sway to turn financial for the events.

It has proposed spending cuts that could result in the loss of billions of dollars in investments and speculations for unstable networks. The plan for spending will wipe out this fund. U.S. Division of the Treasury's Community Development Financial

Institutions Fund which provides billions of dollars of funding through low-paying networks which includes over $300 million for countries in addition to Native American people group, similar to it does with the Economic Development Administration and the Manufacturing Extension Partnership, costing at least another $300 million each year to invests resources in the development of networks. Without the support of the government improvements in financial performance in these areas will continue as well as independent company growth.

Trump has not kept his promise to release the expense forms. Trump's refusal to reveal his expense forms will leave Americans in doubt regarding whether the assessment changes proposed by him will benefit him or the working Americans. Trump always stated the time he was chosen, the administration would release the expense forms he used. Although at the beginning, he stated that the forms were not available because he was being examined the forms because he was being investigated--a fact that doesn't stop any person from making their money--his adviser, Kellyanne Conway has now declared, "He won't deliver his assessment forms."

Proposed $6.7 billion cuts to networks and lodging programs. The budget plan proposed by President Trump will eliminate all Community Development Block Grant, which is used by 1,265 local networks for major activities, such as instance, Meals on Wheels, rehabilitation of the neighborhood, improvement of moderate accommodations, position preparation, and business expansion. It is also expected that the Housing Choice Vouchers program will also be subject to drastic cuts in funding and will be affected by other projects that provide steady assistance to the elderly and people who have disabilities. As per the Center on Budget and Policy Priorities about 200 families currently not receive a voucher for lodging to pay their rental expenses . They could be in the future be forced to leave the lodging market, that has a huge absence of decent accommodations.

The CBO attacked independent experts on spending in the hope that officials ignore negative effects from their methods. The Trump organization blasted the neutral CBO in an attempt to undermine their assessment of the impact of enacting the ACA in a preemptive manner. The attacks came following the CBO estimated they believed that House ACA repeal bill would cut off the participation of 24 million Americans in 2026. This is crucial to the Trump organization's larger goal to destroy independent information and investigate to accentuate the negative effects their plan could have on families with children.

The speculator insurance industry was sabotaged by the government, making it more difficult to the Securities and Exchange Commission, or SEC to hold Wall Street responsible. A committed and independent Division of Enforcement at the SEC is crucial to ensure affordable and fair financial areas for financial experts. Following it was revealed that there had been a Bernie Madoff embarrassment, Obama agency SEC chair Mary Schapiro made it simpler for Division of Enforcement staff to conduct investigations and to issue summons in order to safeguard speculation and reach the bottom of suspicions of misconduct. The seat Michael Piwowar mysteriously moved back this modification, delaying the SEC from protecting the common speculator from bad conduct in the financial sector. He also has proposed shifting about important developments in transparency for corporations, including regarding the everyday freedoms of stocks and stockpile chains as well as the compensation ratio between CEOs and the middle-laborer.

Proposed cuts to financing for programs that aid in sustaining and promote independent enterprise growth. The spending cuts of President Trump will cut funding for a handful of initiatives that aid groups that have generally low possession rates break the boundaries of being able to become businesspeople, for example, the PRIME special help awards given to small-scale business owners with low pay as well as for example, the Minority Business

Development Agency and Economic Development Adm proposes making 23,000 phone calls not answered by disaster-stricken Americans. President Trump's sluggish financial plan suggested the demise from the Corporation for National and Community Service as well as end AmeriCorps. This critical help program is the primary responsibility of identifying volunteers to assist in disaster preparedness and response.

It was suggested through the reduction of funding for the WIC program. The proposal of President Trump to cut subsidies to the WIC program could put vital food security at risk for several families. At a cost for food of around $513 per person The cuts of $200 million could provide an entire year's worth of food and provide nearly 390,000. interested ladies children, babies and young.

Proposed termination of HOME Development Partnerships Program. Up to this point, HOME has helped more than 1.2 million families gain access to secure and affordable accommodation. In any event this program is now on the President's spending plan hacking list which could compromise the security of lodging for a lot of families.

It was proposed to eliminate NeighborWorks America. NeighborWorks America gives awards to network improvement organizations to assist in the production and maintenance of affordable accommodations. The program created 53,649 jobs and assisted 360,009 families at a an average rate during the last year.

Energy and climate

The proposed slices for energy programs that reserve the money of an individual. The Trump spending diagram calls for the creation of a 5.6 percent cut by large for the U.S. Branch of Energy. This cut, along with additional funding for atomic sanitation and waste elimination which means there will be more extreme cuts for programs designed to create family machines that save the money of family members. The spending plan of President Trump also scuts programs, for instance ARPA-E which helps business owners by providing them with clean moderate energy consumption, as well as it also eliminates the Weatherization Assistance Program, which improves the homes of low-income families by providing protection and energy efficient financial enhancements that help reduce costs for services.

They let a pesticide that is risky to be used regardless of its being an enigma to children's health. Chlorpyrifos is a common garden pesticide that causes neurologic troubles in children who are exposed during the uterus. The EPA's scientists believed that the agency should not use chlorpyrifos following the discovery of dangerous levels of the compound in fruit, such as peaches, oranges and strawberries as well as other organic products. Dow Chemical, probably the most prominent manufacturer of products that use this chemical, provided $1 million to the president's launch board of trustees. They also headed an official advisory group to put together. In March,

President Trump's EPA Director Scott Pruitt dismissed the organization's findings by researchers and refused to stop using the chemical and delayed further action until 2022.

It has completely eliminated pollution norms for power stations and offices of oil and gas. In the last year of his presidency the president Obama established the first historically talking carbon contamination rules for power stations as well as the first methane standards since forever for oil and gas penetration into offices. These guidelines would have reduced the brown haze and sediment contaminants that can trigger asthma attacks and reduced the release of carbon and other gases that contribute to environmental change. On March 28 the 28th, President Trump issued a request to the leader that was a first step towards invalidating these pollution guidelines. This will make the process more difficult for the next presidents set up the back.

It has also proposed cutting EPA projects to clean up the water supply. In February the month of February, the president Trump suggested a budget to the EPA to reduce its funding by 31 percent and its staff by a quarter. The proposal of the president focuses on a handful of mainstream programs, like provincial efforts to clean down areas like the Great Lakes, Gulf from Mexico along with the Chesapeake Bay, including other significant waterways.

The proposed removal of initiatives at the EPA dedicated to preventing children who are exposed to paint that is toxic, and could cause neurological delays. A projected 38 million U.S. homes contain poisonous paint. In 2015 the Centers for Disease Control found that 243,000 children had elevated levels of lead levels in their blood. The chemical information is known as a neurotoxin which can cause permanent nerve damage.

Significantly retracted assurances on taking advantage of the water coal infrastructure. The one of Trump organizations first moves was to repeal the Stream Protection Rule set up by the Obama group to stop coal firms from contaminating the close by streams. The decision to reject this ecological insurance was the first issue for the coal industry at the expense of clean , savoring water coal infrastructures.

Rejected against the principle of pay-off to the delight of the oil industry. President Trump removed an opponent of defilement decision that mandated oil and gas firms to disclose the instalments of foreign governments. When he was C.E.O. at Exxon Mobil, Secretary of State Rex Tillerson had campaigned to end the guidelines set out in the Dodd-Frank Wall Street Reform and Consumer Protection Act.

The government ripped of American citizens and refused to fixing the broken federal coal-renting scheme. Trump's administration has pushed to preserve the exemption clause Obama's group closed, allowing coal companies to take advantage of citizens through allowing them to sell coal from the government owned to their auxiliary companies at a falsely cheap prices and avoid sovereign default charges.

The government has not completed the most thorough review of the coal program for more than 30 years, and simultaneously opening the public to new leases in order to extract coal. The majority of offers are the price is $1 per ton and the public is estimated as losing $1 billion per year in lost eminence installments due to coal deals that were undervalued.

We've suggested significant cuts for the Department of Interior's budget, which would reduce the essential maintenance of our parks, while demonstrating in public of support for the parks. One month ago, after he proposed to eliminate $1.5 billion in the form of 12 percent from the Department of Interior's budget and the president Trump made press secretary Sean Spicer ceremoniously hand a $78,000 check, which was Trump's profit from the first quarter, to Secretary of the Department of Interior

Ryan Zinke to help the National Park Service. The problem is that Trump's announcement includes 0.01 percent from $1.3 billion worth of "basic frameworks to be used for maintenance" which is what the National Park Service earnestly needs.

Removed the carpet the private financial specialists who support preservation initiatives. In general chief requests that point toward a defiant reversal of decisions the Obama agency made to tackle the issue of climate change The President Trump has canceled the official announcement which favored private ventures when engineers tackle impacts on particular assets. This is a stumbling block to the natural and financial picks up that the rapidly growing reclamation industry has seen up to as much as $1.15 billion, which is between 2014 and 2015. This is private capital to put resources into territory preservation and water the top executives. The relatively new natural commercial centers rely on the consistency of administration which President Obama's warning was a reminder.

They declared open season on children bears, two-timers and bears. The president Trump changed a law which had protected mountain bear mothers and their offspring from being hunted within their caves. This was because the Obama group's "Reasonable Chase" policy was applicable to shelters for natural life in Alaska as well as a ban on hunting, bewildering and the use of airplanes to hunt and shoot bears and wolves.

Use guidelines on air quality for the air quality guidelines that apply to ozone. Ozone pollution is an essential supporting factor for brown haze that can trigger more frequent asthma attacks and increase the severity of lung diseases. The president's E.P.A. is moving towards changing the standards for air quality that were established under the Obama organization , allowing greater ozone pollution. Ozone contamination at ground level can cause the frequency of asthma attacks and cause windedness, which can trigger the lungs, and lead to permanent damage to the lungs.

The move was made to debi ugh's large-scale openness. Ozone levels that are elevated are linked to an increase in hospitalizations visits to trauma centres as well as unexpected deaths and could cause articulated health effects in children and the elderly.

The president issued a major request to invalidate the "social cost that carbon pollution incurs." President Trump confirmed that environmental change is not a cost by using an important test to assess the benefit of reducing carbon pollution.

Halted decides to limit the discharge of poisons from power stations. Trump's E.P.A. has halted the principles that restrict the unloading of toxic substances for example, arsenic and mercury, as well as pollution from power plants into public waters. This would have been the most important assurances over the past 30 years to manage the spread of poisons and other contaminants in power plants.

New principles were introduced to protect wildlife and water from the harms of lead. After hours of riding a pony his first day of work Secretary of Interior Interior Zinke changed his mind about the restriction that led projectiles to chase in the natural life. The lead content in these photos can cause harm to water and wild life.

They helped in reducing methane pollution norms. The president signed a request to coordinate the E.P.A. along with the Bureau of Land Management to examine the methane pollution guidelines for gas and oil boring offices, and then decide if to change or cancel them. Methane contamination can cause a global temperature change 86 times the amount of carbon contamination.

Discovered a way of turning around the current progress regarding U.S. arrangements for environmental changes. President Trump made a statement in response to a leader's request by rescinding the previous chief privileges associated in the establishment of an environment-friendly U.S. for ecological change and empowering private interests in efforts to lessen the impact of pollution and ensuring that security policies for public safety take into account the effects of environmental change.

He has assigned an E.P.A. overseer who prevents an eye on the environment to prevent modifications. E.P.A. Administrator Pruitt declared to in the media that he does not believe carbon dioxide is the primary driver of environmental change. Pruitt's assertion is based on an air science analogy that says the earth is flat.

Proposed spending cuts could see 5.7 million people with low incomes suffer from the burden of their heating costs, and about 673,000 go without cooling assistance. The proposal of President Trump to phase off the low-income Home Energy Assistance Program, also known as L.I.H.E.A.P., will be especially difficult since more states are experiencing extreme weather.

The system of voting based on votes and the changes to the government

They've harmed American voters with false claims concerning illegal democratic. President Trump's inconsistent allegations of endless misrepresentation undermine the credibility of our races and provide the basis for electoral concealment efforts that threaten our traditional right to have an interest in our own self-government. If government officials spread falsehoods that cast doubt on the legitimacy of our races people lose faith in the voting process. Instead of reacting to obvious threats of a new obstructions and attempts to block the majority of American citizens from submitting their voting documents, Trump decides to spread unverified defamation and demands the pursuit of witches against American citizens.

They've brought debasement of pay-to play to the Trump administration. The Trump family is constantly advancing their business interests both at both home and abroad, while gaining of the government. Defilement, and even the existence of defilement lowers confidence in the government and increases the negative perception of establishments that have a reputation for popularity. If 75 percent of Americans currently believe that corruption runs far and wide in the government President Trump's clear disdain for morals-based rules and the establishment of limitations on official enhancement undermine the popularity-based standard and threatens our system of majority rules economics, public health, and security.

He has undermined the simplicity and accountability by hiding his assessment forms as well as retaining White House guest logs. As he is unable to provide assessments, the complete amount of Trump's responsibility and unknown traps remain undiscovered. So, Americans can't be sure that Trump does not show kindness and unorthodox treatment to his coworkers or that foreign governments and institutions don't have any influence on the Trump organisation and its decisions. It's a mystery to Trump to be the one who leads a campaign to alter the duty code with out Americans being aware of how his plan will benefit his pockets. Modifying the training program to stop the disclosure of White House guest logs keeps society from understanding who is supplying government officials consistently, and also keeps the extraordinary impact of interest obscured.

Migration

Two Muslim and exile boycotts the two boycotts have been imposed by government courts. The first was in January and again in March Trump celebrated the president's Trump declared leader orders prohibiting foreigners from seven and, later in turn, six Muslim-majority countries for at most three months and putting an end to the program of exile for a long period of time. The chief request of January sparked wide-ranging disputes at air terminals across the globe. The request was blocked immediately by a state court in Washington state, followed by the 9th Circuit Court of Appeals. In the first week of March Trump issued a barely updated modification of the initial request, which the courts of Hawaii and Maryland recognized as validly establishing an Muslim as well as exile-based boycott. The central elements in the protest were necessary to be put off.

They focused on every employee who was not approved, but paying little consideration to the values. In the context of high priority given to assets, the Obama group focused its immigration policy on real threats to safety and wellbeing in the same way as border crossings. After a quick start, Trump marked a leader request that outlined the Obama requirements, by focusing on foreigners who are not approved for extradition, giving no attention to how long they've lived living in the United States and their connections to family members and social networks, as well as their different beliefs. In the end, this is a sign that certain people, such as Guadalupe Garcia de Rayos, parent of the family from Arizona who have been living within U.S. for over twenty years. U.S. for more than 20 years, as well as Maribel Trujillo Diaz who is a mom of 4 U.S. conceived youngsters had been extradited.

The foreigner has made victims of domestic abuse and rape unwilling to seek legal to seek help. Forceful migration implementation by the Trump organization--remembering a case for El Paso, where movement authorities captured a casualty of homegrown maltreatment at a town hall after she got a defensive request against her victimizer--has made outsiders and Latinos, paying little heed to migration status, progressively hesitant to approach to report wrongdoings. Investigators in Denver were forced to dismiss four aggressive conduct in home arraignments, since there are no outsiders involved in the case and aren't keen on coordinating. Another incident of violence at the home arraignment in Austin is in an in-between state , under circumstances that are comparable. Since last year, Los Angeles has seen reports from Latinos of rape decrease by 25%, and Houston is expected to see the words of Latinos of assaults decrease by nearly 43 percent. In focusing on everyone this organization has concentrated on no one to the detriment of security for the public.

The Department of Homeland Security has captured a variety of recipients of Deferred Action for Childhood Arrivals (or D.A.C.A. Despite the fact that Trump has declared that he'll handle young non-approved immigrants by displaying "extraordinary determination," also though Secretary of Homeland Security John F. Kelly would like to declare that the man is "the most important thing that has happened in the history of D.A.C.A.," the Department of Homeland Security has been able to limit in any case five recipients of D.A.C.A.--which provides qualified youth with an extradition-free period of two years and a job grant since getting back to work. It has continued to include Daniela Vargas, Daniel Ramirez, Edwin Romero, Josue Romero as well as Francisco Rodriguez. The current account indicates by The Department of Homeland Security ousted Dreamer Juan Manuel Montes while shielded from extradition by D.A.C.A.

They've taken steps to eliminate basic security funding from alleged asylum-seekers' destinations. In the context in the

25th of January's principal request for inside migration requirements and the President Trump made steps to eliminate federal assets from over 600 asylum-related purviews, which hinder participation through bureaucratic authorization. On March 27, Attorney General Jeff Sessions took steps to discredit Department of Justice concedes that it is a part of its mission to assist local law requirements in combating assault weapons, the posse and weapons and to stop the illegal abuse. The comments of the head legal officer were immediately rejected and rebuked by both authorities such as the Fraternal Order of Police and the International Association of Chiefs of Police. Examining the data shows that areas with safe-haven structures have lower crime percent and have more stable economics than those that do not have the strategies.

Afraid approved settlers are prevented from being eligible for benefits and medical treatment that they and their children are entitled. Just a few hours after the Trump group began to work the draft leader's request spilled out, revealing that the group was planning to target lawful settlers who reside inside the United States. The draft request will make legitimate, long-lasting residents of the country, also known as green card holders eligible for extradition in the unlikely chance they take advantage of any of the methods that have been tested to gain advantage from different arrangements. As with the expanded implementation of migration the possibility of the request's improbability has slowed the nation's networks. In California for example for instance, the Alameda County Community Food Bank has seen 40 families withdraw their food stamps, while another 54 eligible families choose not apply to receive food stamps. A variety of reports indicate that some settlers have removed their name from the list to avoid equations for infants or remove children from the child care center.

Confidence

He violated the fundamental freedoms of Muslims through his efforts to create illegal travel boycotts. President Trump's January 27 main event on evacuees, and the reviewed the March 6 leader's activities that was planned to ban entry into the United States for nationals of the Muslim world's greater part and at a fundamental level, restructure the exile affirmations program in order to arrange the case of Christians. Trump's actions have polarized the Muslims people in within the United States and worldwide, damaging their primary relationships with public security allies.

She attempted to redefine strict freedom only for people who have moderate Christian faith. From anti Muslim travel boycotts to the astonishing Holocaust denial statements, the organization can be a threat to the rights of minorities, many of which are ineffective against the escalating instances of hostility towards Semitism and also against Muslim dogmatism.

Vows to decimate the Johnson Amendment, which forestalls philanthropic associations--including places of love--from embracing political competitors. A draft leader's request that was spit out exposes plans to enshrine strict exemptions to government discrimination insurances, revealing an instance of attempts to change the basic notion of a rigorous chance so that it only guarantees people of faith who adhere to moderate Christian beliefs.

The anticipation of firearm violence

A law has been passed that weakens the personal investigation framework of guns and shatters the requirement of current law , which bars individuals suffering from a mental illness from owning guns. By utilizing the alternate method process that is part of the Congressional Review Act, President Trump removed an Social Security Administration guideline that established the procedure by which the office can provide, the National Instant Criminal Background Check System in relation to N.I.C.S., the names of those who -- due to an actual psychological disorder--are barred from firearm ownership under federal law. This is an important step back from ongoing efforts at the state and federal levels to be more likely implementation of the current law, ensuring that all denial buyers' documents are provided to N.I.C.S.

It has made it easier for criminals who escape to buy guns. According to the law of the government, an person considered "a crime involving equity" is prohibited from purchasing or possessing firearms. In all likelihood, from 2006 was the year of the criminal, the F.B.I. together with the Bureau of Alcohol, Tobacco, Firearms and Explosives have diverged on the scope of the law and the F.B.I. getting a position that applies to everyone who has an outstanding warrant for capture, while the A.T.F. advocated for a less restrictive translation , which applies only to people who left the state in which the warrant was issued. Because the F.B.I. is the bureau that is responsible for the framework for historical verification the translation of that office won. However, in February 2017 it was announced that the Department of Justice gave new directions to settle this issue through the acquisition of A.T.F. 's perspective and dramatically reducing the group of individuals who have active warrants for criminal activity that are prohibited from purchasing firearms.

Medical services

The A.C.A. was able to be annulled. A.C.A. The cancellation to the A.C.A. could cause a lot of tension and unease for the many families that rely on it to ensure inclusion. The A.H.C.A. could have resulted in around 24 million more people uninsured over the next 10 years, a violation of President Trump's promise to provide coverage for "everyone." It could also have hurt Trump's pledge to not reduce Medicaid.

They sabotage the A.C.A. commercial center. The Trump organisation has shut down the A.C.A. commercial centre , despite its refusal to relinquish its attempts to repeal the law in a formal manner. Furthermore, the refusal to accept without hesitation the cost-sharing lower sponsorships results in massive vulnerability for back-up plans. This risk directly affects the commercial centre , by encouraging that guarantors end the market in 2018 or to increase their costs.

The government has begun to undermine Medicaid. In a letter addressed to the leading representatives , including Secretary from Health and Human Services Tom Price and Centers for Medicare and Medicaid Services Administrator Seema Verma, the group advised states to pursue negative modifications in its Medicaid programs, such as requirements for work and increased cost-sharing.

The incident has made A.C.A. commercial centre enrollment more difficult. In the final days of the most recent free enlistment period and the Trump organisation halted Healthcare.gov advertising on TV and emails for communication, that are crucial aiding people to remember the cutoff date and keeping in line with the schedule. Although a part of this was reinstated following the backlash, a previous Healthcare.gov head's showcase had officially affirmed that the company's activities had slowed the number of people who enlisted by 480,000.

They sacked Title X financing. As part of the Vice-President's tiebreaking vote in the Senate, the Senate took a vote to defy Obama timing securities to Title X suppliers. Trump approved the legislation with a provision that permits states to block Title X subsidizing. Title X financing gives essential educational, regenerative and guiding services associated with contraception and family planning for four million clients each year.

They have reestablished they reinstated the Global Gag Rule. One of Trump's first acts as president was to reinstate the Global Gag Rule, which prohibits U.S. unfamiliar guide beneficiaries from providing any information and references, administrations, or any other information regarding premature births, regardless of whether they are doing an independent source of financing. It is believed that the Global Gag Rule will prompt more mother-to-child passings, unwanted pregnancies, as well as higher rates of fetus removal that is risky.

She suggested cutting the assets of that program. Teen Pregnancy Prevention Program. The Trump financial plan provides an increase of $50 million in the amount of funding to the Teen Pregnancy Prevention Program, that works with organizations all over the United States to actualize proof-based programs that have been proven to work.

She suggested the defunding of Planned Parenthood. The health care bill of President Trump known as known as the A.H.C.A., would defund Planned Parenthood which cared for 2.5 million patients in 2014.

Higher education

The proposal proposes massive cuts to programs to provide more access to school and reasonable for students with lower incomes as well as those who study shading. The spending plan of President Trump included greater than 5 billion dollars in cuts to important projects, which include those that are part of the Pell Grant application as well as the work-study programs, which provide the necessary assets to assist low-paying students manage the increasing cost of school. The budget cuts also target school access programs, including TRIO and GEAR UP that provide aid, like tutoring, coaching and research opportunities to understudies who are low-paying and unique.

Repealed insurances for loan borrower. On March 16th, the Trump organisation announced measures to protect students who are borrowers of understudy loans. It made the process of reimbursement more complicated by allowing obligation collectors to charge a 16.4 cent cost, in any case, when the borrower is willing to comply with the loan within 60 days. On April 11th the Trump organisation shook off the necessary measures to hold the understudy loan servicers accountable for their actions when they are not in the best interest of understudies' benefit. It is widely documented that servicers put the borrowers in reimbursement programs which can make it harder for them to repay their debt.

They were unable to assist students after a crucial tool for loans and financial aid was closed. In March 2017 without warning the I.R.S. and the U.S. Department of Education removed an essential online tool that allows millions of students to request aid and to repay their loans. The failure to inform students about the program could place applicants for financial aid on the verge of losing their access to help to pay for college, and puts students at risk of seeing their monthly payments rise by several dollars.

They put understudies at risk by naming school officials to the top of the list. Robert Eitel, the senior teacher to Secretary of Education DeVos was a member of the group for several years ago before securing work at Bridgepoint Education, a school with a revenue model that has been subject to various government exams. Additionally, Taylor Hansen, a former lobbyist for schools that are revenue driven - whose dad's loan obligation understudy collection group was sued by the Obama group--was a member of the department's "foothold" organization.

Social liberties of understudies are eroded by naming cynics to the top positions in social liberties. The one chosen to provide as wide an information within the Department of Education, Carlos Muniz was able to shield Florida State University against claims that it shielded a prominent quarterback from charges of assault. Additionally, the new head office of the Office for Civil Rights, Candice Jackson, has confirmed that she will be discriminated against for being white, and is branded the people who blamed the president Trump for his attacks and bullying "counterfeit victims."

Education

The plan was to eliminate the financing provided by the government to after-school programs. In the budget of President Trump the organization was focusing on in the 21st Century Community Learning Centers program, which provides $1.2 billion to locations across the country to fund after-school programs for children and families who work. The funding is used to help the needs of more than 1.6 million students who are enrolled in these initiatives.

The idea was to eliminate the subsidy system that was subsidized by the government to improve instructors with their quality. In the President's budget plan the group focuses on Title II of Every Student Succeeds Act that provides $2.4 billion in grants to state and regions for enrollment of instructors, preparation maintenance, preparing and back. This amount is equivalent to a shortfall of 40,000 teacher payments.

She chose the seriously incompetent and hostile to the public schools, Betsy DeVos, as secretary of education. Devotionals' sole experience with training is as an advocate and megadonor who pushes school vouchers based on tuition across the country. Instead of supporting schools funded by the government and the students who attend these schools, she's considered the government-funded training as to be an "impasse."

The president has revoked the Obama organization's guidelines , which ensured school accountability under legislation called the Every Student Succeeds Act. With this Congressional Review Act, Congress as well as President Trump removed the fundamental security as well as a direction to states and regions to implement the law, which has led to an enormous mess at the local and state local level. The Trump organization has also stated that it is taking an ineffective position on implementation with states, opening up the possibility for the forms to be omitted from their obligations to protect insecure understudies.

Repealed the Obama organisation's guidelines, which supported improvement in teacher preparation programs. With the Congressional Review Act, Congress as well as Trump eliminated the state's requirements to ensure that instructor arrangement programs assist aspiring teachers develop the skills that are able to use in the home and support learning understudy. Without these guidelines, the system will continue to be improved for educator readiness initiatives and backing the most effective projects.

It was suggested to cut $9 billion off the government-funded school system and consuming $1.4 billion of school funds on school decisions. This proposal includes destructive vouchers for private schools that are not public as well as the introduction of a $250 million federal program which will allow citizen funds to be redirected to private schools, which aren't accountable, can differ in affirmations and discipline, and are not dependent on crucial oversight, observation, and social freedoms laws.

The idea was to cut immediate assistance to schools in their change initiatives. By focusing on support for the AmeriCorps program President Trump could harm a number of top education associations. From K.I.P.P. Public Charter Schools, teach for America From K.I.P.P. Public Charter School up to City Year have effects affected understudies across the nation and are dependent upon that program.

Equity

They designated Jeff Sessions, a long-lasting adversary of social equality as head of the legal department and the country's most powerful law enforcement officer. The meetings also supported their support for the First Amendment Defense Act, which is a brutal law that prevents the federal government from engaging in "oppressive actions" against any company or individual who has been victimized by L.G.B.T.Q. Individuals. The demonstration hopes to secure the right, with everything else is equal. refuse aid to L.G.B.T.Q. persons who depend on two arrangements that are based on strict convictions.

It is, or should be viewed as the union between a man and one lady.

Sexual relations are a right to be a marriage." In the course of a federal investigation during 1983 Sessions accused a group of voting rights activist to extort money from an elector. As the chief implementationer of the social rights laws in the United States, it is impossible to see how he can currently secure the same network for which Sessions advocated the separation.

Designated Justice Neil Gorsuch, an adjudicator with an extensive record of deciding against the rights of laborers women, understudies, and ladies who have disabilities -- to the Supreme Court. Equity Gorsuch will rule on the key issues of the issue of social equality, cash-in legislation, and conceptual rights. In the near future, for instance he'll decide if the Court should let the state's democratic bill of 2013--which the lower court said was targeted people of color with "practically meticulous precision"and should remain in the end.

They pressured the Senate to make the "atomic option" to have the Supreme Court chosen one affirmed. Nearly every else equity in the Court was supported by a bipartisan majority. It was able to pass the 60-vote limit at some point or the other during the affirmation process. However, many congressmen disagreed with Trump's preferred method. Alternative atomic strategies Senate pioneers have now been in a position to confirm Trump's established appointed officials by an essential and more important component.

The authenticity of the court's structure. As a president and applicant, Trump has assaulted decides whom he does not respect for, and has ruined the courts' credibility. Trump called an appointed official who ruled on his prejudicial Muslim boycott as a "purported Judge." During the visit the judge said that an American-Mexican judge couldn't be impartial when claiming against Trump due to his ethnicity. The attacks on the third tier of government undermine the originators detachment of forces as well as the same law-related guidelines.

They assigned philosophical fanatics the courts of the government. The Trump group is the moment confirming moderate ideologues' give their names to government courts. Trump's picks, especially for the Fifth Circuit Court of Appeals are a clear indication of a determined effort to alter the legal executive's philosophies. Trump has well over 100 seats to fill due to Senate obstruction during Obama's presidency. Trump as of late has declared that the group is not going to seek out the advice of The neutral American Bar Association.

It was suggested to dispose of the Legal Services Corporation. In effect, a slender admission to equity is put out than the reach of 60.6 million low-paying Americans as a result of President Trump's plan to end the Legal Services Corporation, which is the country's crucial subsidizing transfer for the regular lawful administrations.

However, they were was not done to hinder Baltimore police efforts to change. The head of the legal department Sessions demanded a court not to recognize an assent decree that was accepted by the Baltimore police mayor, city hall head as well as network members and professionals Department of Justice lawyers. The federal Court denied Sessions's movement, and allowed the police to make changes that are required for building confidence between police officers and networks that they manage to be carried out.

They were attempting to revive the fight with drugs. The outdated method proved ineffective and led to the annihilation of long-distance relationships for many families. Chief Legal officer Sessions is a ferocious method of addressing wrongdoing to increasing government arraignments as well as long sentences of imprisonment in any case for peaceful, low-level criminals. In fact, when the Trump organisation pushes outdated laws, Democratic and Republican lead representatives are increasing their support for opposing changes, drug treatment and alternatives to detention.

He supported outdated and ineffective criminal equity reforms thatdisproportionately impact networks of shade. The principal legal officer Sessions should focus on the necessity for change in the police force, assisting new methods for reducing wrongdoing, as well as ensuring that drug treatment alternatives to prison are readily available. If all else is equal Sessions has asked for an audit of the current examples and instances of police misconduct where evidence and an extensive report have revealed that the police officer acted in violation of the law. He also has addressed many years of scientific and examination rejecting an extreme on-wrongdoing strategy.

They reformed the Obama time Department of Justice's structure and stopped contracting with private jails. Private prisons can be a naive incentive to detain more people as they're driven to increase the amount of benefit they receive, by the fact that more detainees are occupying their facilities. Private detention facilities that are contracted with the Department of Justice were discovered to be less effective and also have higher security, as well as the board has issues.

Equity in race

They have defended financial policies that hinder the networks of shading. The majority of budget reductions that President Trump would reduce basic social aid programs. For example, 41 percent out of 9 million women, Infants, and Children which is also known as W.I.C., beneficiaries are minorities. The budget plan also dispensates of minorities. Minority Business Development Agency, encouraging business growth for people of non-white backgrounds, which is the fastest growing population segment.

It has backed education policies that don't help students of people of color. The Trump group supports slices of Pell Grants and educational cost assistance projects as well as parts of after-school programs which could impact one out of four African American understudies. The group also promotes voucher programs that don't aid the achievement of students of color.

It has pushed natural strategies that adversely impact shading networks. As has been proven the years, the E.P.A. is required to eliminate all programs dedicated to reducing the openness of lead paint and lopsidedly regulating shading networks. The E.P.A. is also cutting subsidies for the office of ecological equity which was recently set in order to handle lead contamination in particular, as well as other challenges facing systems of shade.

L.G.B.T.Q.

They've deliberately ignored the unlawful opposition to transsexual segregation in schools. The Trump group has resisted Title IX direction by the Department of Education explaining schools are obligated under long-standing federal law on social liberties to treat transsexual understudies in the same way and with dignity. Transsexual students are subject to constant harassment and a lack of respect in schools and impedes their ability to learn. About one of every six transsexual students in K-12 have been evicted from schools due to this nagging.

Removed L.G.B.T.Q. individuals from studies in administrative which made it difficult to determine if government programs can help them in a decent way. The Trump organization has eliminated questions about L.G.B.T.Q. People who are subject to government scrutiny regarding projects that help people with disabilities and seniors Without this, politicians and their supporters aren't able to assure L.G.B.T.Q. Individuals are also eligible to join the most important organizations funded by taxpayers, for instance, Meals on Wheels. It is also believed to have included, but then retracted and omitted inquiries about L.G.B.T.Q. People who participated in those who participated in the American Community Survey, a annual study that collects data regarding Americans fulfilling their education as well as their lodging and health participation.

They identified long-term adversaries of L.G.B.T.Q. Rights--including people who are opposition to L.G.B.T.Q. Refrain from gatherings, including key positions within organizations. Many of the Trump's Cabinet members including the Attorney General Jeff Sessions and Secretary of Health and

Human Services Tom Price were able to fulfill their duties by blocking the flow of L.G.B.T.Q. Rights. Now, they're accountable for organizations that have authority over these rights. The arrangement is quite shocking the more you study: Trump tapped Ken Blackwell who was previously an opposition to L.G.B.T.Q. as a local approach guide to select the members of the group known as C-FAM for his presidency for the United Nations; and delegated Roger Severino, a long-term antagonist of transsexual equality, to head his own Department of Health and Human Services' Office for Civil Rights.

It has suggested cutting funding for HIV/AIDS research in order to find a cure. President Trump has proposed cutting portions of wellbeing research and incorporating $6 billion parts for the National Institutes of Health in the spending plan , and an additional $50 million for the Centers for Disease Control and Prevention's H.I.V. Research anticipation programmes. The organization also increased its budget by $300 million on the

President's Emergency Plan for AIDS Relief (or P.E.P.F.A.R... This highly successful program offers an lifesaving treatment to 11.5 million people around the world and offers a wide array of bipartisan support.

Refuge searchers and evacuees who are banned escape from L.G.B.T.Q. Security mistreatment throughout America. United States. President Trump's suspension of evacuees hindered L.G.B.T.Q. Syrian and Iraqi refugees from finding refuge inside America. United States, leaving them to be stranded in countries that abuse them. The strategy of encirclement prevents all refugees who cross the southern border and keeps the number of people who are focusing on extradition traps L.G.B.T.Q. Haven seekers in dangerous areas of settler confinement increase the risk that they could be unlawfully extradited to any of the countries in which their lives are at risk. The organization also decided to close the sole dedicated transsexual migrant detention unit within the country, putting transsexuals who are detained at risk.

Security for the public

We've caused Americans less secure from Islamic State as well as I.SI.S. The Trump organization's ally in Muslim fanaticism has made every American less secure, as it aids I.S. and other psychologically militant gatherings attract supporters. One I.S. leader in Afghanistan stated that according to one Afghan leader, the Trump organization's "utter disdain for Muslims can make our work much easier due to the fact that we could recruit thousands." First, the Muslim boycott involved Iraq and Afghanistan, where an Iraqi officer fighting close to U.S. powers against I.S.I.S. was deemed to be a "double-crossing."

They've resulted in Americans less able to fight the spread of pandemic diseases, such as, Zika and Ebola. Massive reductions in the guidelines health, discretion, and well-being suggested in the President's F.Y. 2017 spending plan will end the Global Health Security account, which helps identify, prevent, and treat infectious diseases across the globe including Ebola. In his budget proposal, Trump has also called to end funds for the Fogarty International Center, which helps fund initiatives in global health research that include infectious disease research in the developing world.

He has undermined American position and security through transferring worldwide management to Beijing. The president Trump has made no efforts to achieve a more balanced relationship with China. He has sloppyly played with the idea of upsetting more than 40 years of an strategy of "one China" yet threw out the window on his first phone call to the Chinese president, signalling that his fears were not real. Trump along with Secretary of State Rex Tillerson guaranteed they would keep China from expanding its reach on the disputed areas located in the South China Sea. But, China continues to do what it wants, wherever it requires. Trump's summit with the Chinese president Xi Jinping at his Mar-a-Lago resort didn't result in any advancement in any controversial issue. Beijing is adamant about Washington as a flimsy rumor with no substance. Trump's"all talk method of no activity allows for restraint over opportunities and ensures tyrant pioneers that the suppression of their ideas will continue.

They have controlled an increase in the number of non-military personnel who are being removed out of U.S. military tasks. After a long period of decline, non-military personnel suffering losses as a result of U.S. military activities have increased under Trump and have destroyed families, destabilizing crucial points, and providing publicity to U.S. foe. U.S. military representative Col. Joseph Scrocca said "[More non-military personnel deaths] are likely to weaken the effectiveness the alliance. In addition, it is what ISIS is trying to stop in the present." Civilians' passing's across Iraq and Syria have increased significantly in 2017, almost surpassing the total for the year 2016. Trump's first major strike as president at Yemen during January made during dinner in the White House, which was away from the normal cycle and resulted in a number of regular citizens passing's.

The attack on public security has hurt the credibility of America's majority-rule government through a steady lack of transparency and refusing to reveal the truth about the sources of his money and his ties to Russia. Americans don't know to whom Trump is owing money to, or what Trump could owe cash to or what obligations the group may require from Russia or other forces that aren't familiar to him. Trump's reluctance to speak out against the Russian government's interference in the 2016 election and to discharge his forms for assessment; moving away from his business and embracing a free commission and extraordinary insight to see the less significant part of Russia's role in the 2016 election can be interpreted as a green light for Russians as well as other groups that have the right to enter into U.S. the majority rule system. All Americans of all ideologies are vulnerable when a foreign influence, cash, and hacking is allowed to run amok on America's popular-based basis.

Chapter 12: How Did The Donald Trump Administration Fail The U.S. Citizens

There are a myriad of reasons that United States citizens don't want Trump as President any more.

Trump's immigration policy is a failure in the eyes of Supreme Court. Supreme Court.

A decision that was very close A very close decision: the U.S. Supreme Court has confirmed the protection from deportation of individuals who have been in U.S. U.S. since children without documents.

U.S. President Donald Trump

The Supreme Court in Washington confirmed the protection from deportation of about 700,000 immigrants who are known as dreamers. They entered the USA illegally as children and their parents. It was the U.S. government's decision to end the program known as the Daca program initiated by U.S. President Donald Trump's predecessor Barack Obama in 2017 was "arbitrary and imprudent," ruled the chief justices. With five judges in the majority, of the nine judges, this decision was too slack. The Conservative Chairman of the Supreme Court, John Roberts was a part of the decision along with 4 Liberal judges.

Trump is in turmoil

President Trump U.S. president described the verdict on Twitter as "terrible" and suggested that it was motivated by politics.

The year 2012 was the time that Obama secured around 700,000 "dreamers" of deportation through the supposed Daca order. A large portion of these were brought to the United States as children by their parents with no papers, mostly coming from Latin American countries. Trump shut down the program in September 2017, but he kept the freeze on deportations for the moment.

Trump has declared the fight against illegal immigration as well as the limitation of legal immigration an important part during his term as president. In the first week in the week majority conservative Supreme Court had made a decision that was in opposition to the policy that was being pushed by the Trump administration. The Supreme Court reinforced the insurance of transsexuals and gay people in the workplace and declared that the exemption of exclusion contingent on sexual orientation or sex-related character was not in accordance with U.S. law.

Majority of voters opposed to Trump

According to a study most Americans are in favor of legalizing immigrants. According to research conducted by Pew Research Centre Pew Research Centre, around three-quarters of adult U.S. citizens favour granting children who entered the country without proper papers an indefinite right to stay. According to Pew the majority of 90 percent of Democratic Party supporters and political independents favor a long-term right to reside in the case of children who have been referred to "Dreamer". Only half of Republican supporters are in favor of legalization.

Trump's relations with the media. Trump does not speak out on Twitter the things that other politicians do. army of lawyers, P.R. agencies, and broadcasters of the regime. Everyone feels badly represented by regime broadcasters and government agencies and everyone is monitored through fake news. Perhaps it's even Merkel. Merkel does not feel that she is treated with respect by ARD. Let it go.

4. Trump's refusal to listen to the news media. Because he's loyal to Roy Moore, for example even though the whole American media has tried to discredit the alleged people who were victims to his crimes come forward the most critical witnesses has to admit that she altered the evidence that was circulated through the world's media. It's time to get over it. It's irritating that the press and president insist on deciding the one who is dishonorable.

5. Trumps mental state. Trump was adamant about this incumbent Roy Moore but then sided with him, unlike the majority of his own party. As you can see, he likely is able to win in Alabama because of it, and the Democrats make their senators take a step back even on allegations that are questionable. Trump might seem to be erratic and impulsive, but he's a gambler as well as a determined fighter who is determined to keep going and hasn't lost his way yet, and has been successful so far. Let it go.

6. Trump's impeachment. The New Republic a fantastic and widely read argument to the conclusion Impeachment is a simple idea, but isn't going to be the case, it's a matter of getting over it, and is based on the political process. Many people, including Democrats might also appreciate this article because it is a departure of that "lock Trump down" desire to witness Trump in court , as reported by the international press.

7. Trump's tendency to take action is a bit odd to think that Trump did something that had been announced prior to his announcement. This is not typical for Western politicians, who typically are waiting until there is an alternative to their actions. The president Obama could have implemented measures like bans on automatic guns, but chose to avoid and compromise on the cultural wars which Trump proves can be solved from the opposite side. Learn from it.

8. What Celebrities are saying about Trump. Harvey Weinstein was against Trump. Bill Clinton was against Trump. Lena Dunham, who warned Hillary Clinton about Weinstein, was anti Trump and was planning to quit the country if Trump was elected. Arnold Schwarzenegger was against Trump and had a MeToo issue. The Bush were also against Trump and have their own questions. The majority of journalists and artists who were fired from MeToo were against Trump. MeToo series were in opposition to Trump. Kevin Spacey was against Trump. Perhaps, having a stance

opposed to Trump simply brings bad luck since everyone is in opposition to Trump. The headlines are cheap and made with these famous witnesses, yet they rely on the media to get rid of those who might not be much more or less than Trump also. Be over them.

9. The polls are on Trump. The pre-election polls all were incorrect. Every assessment of the reality of politics were incorrect. Perhaps Trump simply has an understanding of the people who can win or lose the elections as well as what they're looking for and what motivates people to vote. I'm assuming that, in an German journalist's study, 91% of the population are against the American Embassy in Jerusalem. However, American Jews vote in unison in the United States, and up to the 1980s, they nearly constantly voted for explosive-proof Israeli-loyal Democrats. Trump might have provoked three days of anger in Palestine those who are always searching for reasons to feel angry and are not casting a vote in America. That's the way people in the American Jews see it. The idea that an

Democratic candidate might resign and would likely do it in order to please the extremist left and Jews-haters such as Linda Sansour or Black Life's Matter who supported the Democrats during the Obama timeframe - the thinking is to turn a segment who are voting to Republicans. Because of MeToo and the BDS initiative and MeToo the phrase "old white males" has had an anti-Semitic taste. I've written and worked with this group for a long time; I've met their names and can only say: Let's get over it. You can also ask yourself when the next election comes around, if Trump is going to do better on both the west and east coasts next time. Since the year 1995, presidential administrations had pledged to change the tone. They didn't follow through with it. Trump has made it happen.

10. Every thing Trump does is posted on Twitter. Trump tweets this on Twitter so that anyone can take it on their own. Yes, he describes an overweight and short North Korean short and fat and possibly in violation of community guidelines and diplomatic norms. I find it hilarious. I

laughed. I'm very entertained in a bizarre way, and I do not need to be constantly reminded with Sam the Eagle to must look up this mix consisting of Gonzo, Fuzzy Bear, Das Tier and Statler and Waldorf bad. Trump isn't Merkel who a few months ago claimed to be the chief of the Free World, and who does a prick in front of the family members and victims of Breitscheidplatz as well as Sigmar Gabriel who sets off an end to the Western bond in his passionate speeches due to the fact that he feel respected by Trump.

Trump frequently praises his army. It's like watching Simpsons and hearing someone shout at me every day to not consider Homer's use beer as well as nuclear fuel stick hilarious. The media is exactly like that, they promote Trump and find it to be disgusting.

After a long time of promises to help ordinary Americans the President's first 100 days have shown the reality of his arrangement requires profit-making partnerships and those with the highest incomes not all to the disadvantage of everyone else. The activities of his organization and those are characterized by broken promises, net irreconcilable circumstances and a clear degrading of morality, honesty and other standards based on votes. Trump, as a candidate, Trump guaranteed the American people that if we were to "... be able to win an amount, "we'll be cautious about losing." But it's not American people who are winning, it's Wall Street, private jails as well as the oil industry as well as Trump's family. A recent Gallup study found that the majority of Americans are currently adamant the fact that the president Trump does not adhere to his responsibilities and is unable to properly manage public authorities.

Chapter 13: The Donald Trump's Demise
Donald Trump

President Trump was losing ground due of his impulsive approach to confront the administration. This is what was promoted by Democrats in the 2020 election. Trump in opposition to Biden is a definite relationship in our current political climate and it's important also, to stop the state of things that could be on the future.

The Republican coalition is concerned about disruption and a decision that is yet to be defined in terms of its severity. Their main concern is the goodwill of things to move forward by relying on past objectives, which could become obsolete over time. The re-established Black Lives Matter development took back the focus to organized racism, which was overlooked for many years in The Republican Party and denied by the President. In addition, Biden vows to achieve improvements and will make promises to tackle this issue within the framework of equity. Furthermore, Joe

Biden's choice to name Kamala Harris to be a "lady of Indian or African source' was like "hitting the center of the ball". The result was that people came out to vote.

In the economy that is not regulated, or, in essence, the free business of and the U.S.A. and its ardent support from The Republican Party shows tax breaks as well as a lack of business regulations. In the same way the president Donald Trump is against American corporations that re-appropriate to countries such as China to return America positions. Trump promised to create ten million jobs in the next 10 months. It was, however, a debate' and there was no conclusion even as the economy grew. Biden's President-Elect plans to increase the government's rates for those with annual earnings of more than $400,000 and to use the funds for public assistance, in addition to increasing Federal the minimum wage allowed by law to $15 per hours (from $7.25).

Concerning COVID following his previous efforts to minimize the COVID-19 epidemic,

Trump finally set aside $10 billion for treatment and improvement of antibody. U.S. pulled out from the WHO and criticized the organization for collaborating relations with China regarding the facts about the origin of Coronavirus. Trump has never really tried to combat COVID. Biden is planning to create the project of contacting following and is planning to reinstate respect for WHO. He has also stated that 'I will be contacting the populace for 100 days before lifting the veil. I think we'll witness an important decrease'

On climate change, a skeptical man that Trump is, he defended unsustainable resources to be used to power age. But it was reported that Trump has announced that U.S. pulled out from the Paris Climate Accord when he was first elected President. U.S.A. is expected to leave at the date of the end of 2020. Biden has assured American citizens that he will be a part of the accord when his term begins and intends to oppose any new rents that are imposed for shale gas and oil permeating open land. Biden intends to work with to see the U.S.A. to arrive at net-carbon emission-free in 2050 by investing $2 trillion into environmentally-friendly power generation.

In terms of international strategy the biggest flaw of Trump's international strategy is his pledge to reduce U.S. troop levels abroad or to invest more resources into the military. In the meantime Trump failed to make progress on the North Korea harmony bargain and left the Iran bargain and then stumbled trying to broker a deal between India as well as Pakistan. In recent times, he has accelerated his efforts. Biden has not made many harmony agreements that are in this region. Middle East among Israel and U.A.E., Bahrain, Sudan identified for one of the Abraham Accords. But, Biden has been more conscious of his duties and has been portrayed as the great things that have had been achieved.

Exchanges have been another major feature in Trump's Trump system. Biden announced a tougher tax on China and even item-specific ones against the other Asian nations, and is testing global alliances that appear to be in opposition to U.S. interests. Biden assures that he will eliminate one-sided taxation placed by China through Trump. Trump Administration. If all else is equal take steps to establish the global community that instead hold China to be accountable.

In the end this wacky way to approach strategies and administration was the cause of Trump's downfall, and his admiration for Twitter. But, even the Biden is the President-elect Biden is making plans for his administration , he has designated several individuals to his administration, Trump keeps on perplexing the world with his accusations of blatant as well as a wide-ranging misrepresentation of the American public and refuses to accept that his loss. While the President-elect Joe Biden has arisen the plausible winner, following the approval of most of the 270 appointed decisions on December 14 , 2020, the pause and watch game must be played until he takes an official pledge to become the 46th President to America. United States of America.

It is believed that the Democratic Presidential campaigner Joe Biden won the U.S. election based on consensus forecasts in the vital Pennsylvania state. Pennsylvania. The A.P.A.P. news agency as well as CNN, N.B.C., C.B.S. and A.B.C. and A.B.C. declared the former Vice President the winner in this hotly debated duel with the incumbent Donald Trump. Trump becomes the 46th president to be elected in U.S. history.

The event was preceded by a major competition to make up with the count of votes. Trump was ahead by nearly 600,000 vote the morning of Wednesday (local local time). This was due to the fact that in Pennsylvania the ballots cast on elections day were first counted and the vast majority of voters were a vote for Trump. Early voters who were more likely to choose Biden were not analyzed until afterward.

In a address for the country, Joe Biden emphasized that his victory was an "clear" as well as "convincing" victory in the election. In Wilmington the Democrat declared that the time for healing was upon us. He was now president of Unity. In his speech he said his belief that the U.S.A. ought to be redeemed in the world. In his address to Trump fans, he explained that he was sorry for their displeasure. He's suffered defeats of his own. "Let's give each other a chance" he declared. It's time to put the savage and heated exchanges to the side.

The Vice President of the future Kamala Harris took the stage first and thanked voters. They would have chosen hope and decency, unity and science "and the truth, indeed". "Although it is my first time to be in this position, I'll never be the only one," Harris said. Harris.

In the shadow of in the White House in Washington, DC Many young women are celebrating the achievements in the life of Kamala Harris. Kamala Harris is the first female Vice President in the United States and also the first African-American woman to be Vice President. Her father hails originally from Jamaica as is her mom hails from India. "It's amazing to have the first female vice president and black women who is of Indian origin," said Anuja Mur. "We're very excited as our family is all from South Asia too." The friend of hers Roshi Desai told her she was excited about "finally sleeping" after waiting for days to hear the outcome of the elections.

The youngest of the women of this group Anamika Satsangi equally happy that a brand new administration is taking over the White House: "Then we'll find someone who is a good listener to research and treats COVID with respect," she said. However, she is aware, "that not all problems will be resolved immediately by the new president, but it's an important move towards an upward direction."

Vice-Chancellor Olaf Scholz considers the tight election result as well as the U.S.A.'s opposition to the election as warning signs to Germany. In a guest piece in the newspaper "Bild at Sunday" which is owned by the S.P.D. Politiker wrote that the incident was not just an action-packed political drama that lasted for days, but was also a warning of where it could take us if our society were to split. The U.S.A. there is not only the difference between the wealthy and the wealthy that separates the nation. There is a growing gap between the city dwellers and rural populace. "In Germany, too, we see that the society is changing. Many feel like people who are not worthy of their place," declared Finance Minister Federal. Finance.

U.S. President Donald Trump's campaign team has announced an action throughout the presidential election in Arizona. In the lawsuit, certain residents from the Maricopa district were provided with incorrect instructions from election officials to use their voting devices. These issues could be vital for the result of this election in the state which has eleven electorates.

Black Lives Matter Square inside the White House in Washington, DC transformed into a one-party as Joe Biden's win in the presidential election became the talk of the town. The crowd gathered in glorious autumn weather, cheered , dancing in the street, and enjoyed champagne. Bri Gillis is a young lady who hails from Washington, DC, even presented the Biden supporters champagne shower. "It is so great to awake in the morning without having to be concerned whether the President might be tweetingabout," Gillis exclaimed, trying to block out the applause of the crowd. "I'm thrilled to have Madame the Vice-President Kamala Harris as well. It was due to her that I chose Democrats." Democrats."

Many of the high-rises located in New York have their tips shine in American flag colors after that the U.S. election results were released. At the very top, the Empire State Building shone on Sunday evening in red, white and blue. It was in celebration of the election victories from Joe Biden and Kamala Harris as announced by the owners. There were many other skyscrapers like that of Bank of America skyscraper and the Bloomberg Tower in Manhattan were also lit up.

The Federal Minister for Economics Peter Altmaier warns of exaggerated expectations of U.S. election winner Joe Biden in the field of economics. The severe tariffs on aluminum as well as steel that Trump are Donald Trump are "not off the table," says the CDU politician. "Certain businesses in U.S. have become more competitive as a result of the tariffs that are punitive, as the prices have been artificially raised. Joe Biden will not be comfortable with this either."

U.S. President Donald Trump has declared himself to be the winner of the presidential election again regardless of U.S. broadcasters and data providers who's estimates. "I was the winner, I had 71,000,000 legal vote," he wrote on Twitter. "Bad events have occurred which our observers were not permitted to observe," he explains without giving any proof. "That was never before." Twitter immediately issued Trump an alert: "The allegation of election fraud is controversial," it said. Trump has claimed - without providing any evidence to prove that there was a massive election fraud that occurred on Tuesday.

The Federal Minister of Foreign Affairs Heiko Maas stated: "The way in which Donald Trump governed and how his actions abroad have caused us a lot of issues." Maas also said to the "Bild" publication that there are "some issues that have to be adjusted within the transatlantic relationship and I'm certain that working with Joe Biden that will work out nicely." Maas declared via Twitter on Twitter that Germany is eager to work with the new U.S. government. "We would like to invest in cooperation to create a new transatlantic partnership and the so-called New Deal."

Iranian Vice-President Eshaq Jahangiri said he hoped for a shift in "destructive political machinations" that has been taking place in the United States after Joe Biden's election victory. Jahangiri also hoped for the return of the law, international obligations and respect for all nations. "The period of Trump and his daring and warmongering group is over.

The media around the world reacts to the outcome of the election. Many commentators are relieved and express hope that Biden can "restore the faith" ("Neue Zurcher Zeitung"). "The catastrophe was avoided," writes the British Guardian. Its French paper "Le Monde" felicitates Biden for the "victory of an emancipated survivor". Biden is "a president who could create a tension among the U.S. and the world," believes "El Mundo" from Spain.

Joe Biden the 7th of November is today a significant day in a variety of ways. Exactly 48 years ago, he was selected as a senator to Senate Senate as the first senator. A half century after that, Biden can crown his political career. And, in turn, Trump is the first president ever since George HW Bush to be removed from office within a single term and the fourth President since the ending the end of World War II. In the meantime, if Trump is legally unsuccessful in his plan to challenge the presidency, Trump can live in the White House and fly on the president's Air Force One aircraft. But, he's now being referred to as a "lame duck" (literally: "lame duck") or being deemed to have lame wings. However, he is still able to be a dictator and even hold administrative positions in the administration.

The well-known Republican senator Mitt Romney does not just congratulate Democrats Joe Biden and Kamala Harris, but praises them as "people who are good-willed and have an admirable character". The political figure who is a religious one tweets his followers on Twitter: "We pray that God will be with you in the coming days and years to follow." Romney is widely regarded as a critic for the current president Trump.

Tens of thousands U.S. citizens celebrate Biden's victory in the presidential election. In Washington Biden's supporters throng towards the White House to celebrate the Biden's victory over the incumbent. Similar scenes are seen within New York, where Trump established his headquarters as real estate investor.

NATO Secretary General Jens Stoltenberg looks ahead after some rifts within the alliance during Trump's time in office: U.S.

leadership is more important than ever. Stoltenberg is looking forward to a closer relationship with the newly elected president and his deputy in order to "further improve the ties with North America and Europe with the new administration".

A number of Democratic former presidents in the United States join the well-wishers Trump's predecessor Barack Obama writes: "I could not be happier." In reference to the deep division in this US, Obama explains that everyone has to take action to "lower the temperature and come to an agreement on how for moving forward." Bill Clinton writes: "America has spoken, and democracy has prevailed." The 96-year-old Jimmy Carter, who served up to 1981 as president He is thrilled to witness the "positive shifts" in the direction Biden as well as Harris "will be bringing to the country.

French president Emmanuel Macron congratulates on Twitter and anticipates: "We have a lot to do in order to face the challenges of the present. Let's join forces!" Trump's anti-European rhetoric has been a problem for fierce European Macron's camp during the last few years.

The leaders of the European Union, the E.U.E.U. Conseil President Charles Michel and E.U.E.U. Commission chief Ursula van der Leyen, wish both the "elected vice president" along with"Elected Vice President "elected vice-president". Von der Leyen also wrote that she is eager to meet Biden soon as she can. "Together" Europe and the U.S.A. have "built an unparalleled transatlantic partnership" built on "freedom as well as human rights as well as social justice along with an open economic system" and remains "a foundation for stability as well as security and prosperity" between the two sides on the Atlantic.

The Federal president Frank-Walter Steinmeier also congratulates Biden and assures Biden of the close relationship between Germany and Biden. "Your presidency will bring together the hopes of millions of people far from the boundaries of your own country and even those in Germany," Steinmeier wrote to Biden. "It is the chance to find finding a new consensus. It's the promise of trust, common sense and the ongoing effort to find solutions to a turbulent world." Biden is the Federal President points out that Biden represents "for an America that understands the value of friendship and alliances as well as trust and reliability.

The Chancellor Angela Merkel congratulates on the victory of the. Merkel is excited about "future collaboration between Biden," writes Merkel on Twitter. Biden," writes Merkel on Twitter. "Our transatlantic relationship is unalterable for us to tackle the challenges that face us in our times.

Joe Biden wants to address the nation with a speech at 22:00 a.m. C.E.T.

British Premier Secretary Boris Johnson congratulates Biden and Harris for their victories. It is worth noting that the U.S. is the U.K. primary ally, and Johnson looks forward to working closely with them.

The newly-elected U.S. President Biden has also won in the critically important state of Nevada According to forecasts from media sources. A news organization A.P.A.P. as well as the T.V.T.V. broadcaster Fox and the T.V.T.V. broadcaster Fox Biden has won the votes of six additional electorates and has strengthened his standing in the coming legal fight regarding the outcome of the election.

The newly elected U.S. Vice President Kamala Harris has assured Americans that she as well as Joe Biden will serve the nation. "This election is more then Joe Biden and me. It's about the soul of America and our commitment to fight for it,"" Harris tweeted. "We have a lot of tasks to accomplish. Let's get started." She becomes the first African-American woman and the first female to hold the position of U.S. Vice President. In a second tweet, she shares an image of her beaming with happiness.

With Joe Biden's victory in the election an era of optimism has begun in the USA according to Pelosi, the House of

Representatives' chairwoman, Democrat Nancy Pelosi. Biden was able to claim an "historic triumph" and is fully prepared to confront the nation's issues from the beginning during his term as president.

Joe Biden's victory in the US presidential election has brought relief to Germany. German Foreign Minister Heiko Maas tweeted via Twitter on Twitter that Germany is eager to work with the new US administration. "We would like to invest in our partnership for a fresh transatlantic partnership, a fresh agreement.

The world breathes a sigh joy," tweeted the CDU politician Friedrich Merz. SPD General Secretary Lars Klingbeil wrote: "Democracy is awesome!" FDP President Christian Lindner was also relieved: "There is a chance of a fresh start in this transatlantic alliance. We Europeans should make the most from it." Left-wing boss Katja Kipping got the surprising positive result with the defeat of candidate Donald Trump in view: "Almost half of the vote were cast by a loud-mouthed liar who was a snob to women, democracy and anyone who tried to defy Trump every single day. "

Trump doesn't recognize Joe Biden's win. "The reality is that the election isn't being over," said the incumbent US president. Biden has been "wrongly" depicting his self as the victor, and is backed with the president's "media supporters". Trump's term as president will be in office until the 20th of January.

Joe Biden has promised to be the "President of All Americans". Biden said he is "honoured" to be chosen to "lead our nation with pride," tweeted Biden. "The task ahead is a challenge however, I can assure that I will be President for the entire population of Americans regardless of whether you've have voted to me for president or not.

A few minutes after a number of US media outlets announced Democratic Presidential candidate Joe Biden the winner of the US election, the crowds erupted in cheers on the streets of New York. Many people cheered, clapped and cheered throughout the duration of the streets or in their windows in their apartments. A lot of drivers honked their horns continuously. The city located on the US east coast is mostly democratic and liberal, however it also happens to be the home of current US President Donald Trump's birthplace.

What happened? Donald Trump Lost The 2020 Election.

The whole thing finally came down to the man. The lies and the outrageous claims along with the confusion and destructive administration, the angry rants, the race-baiting, the predatory tendencies and the need to control everything that led to the making of the president Donald Trump the ringmaster of the American political marketplace finally compelled more of the American population to remove him from the tent.

Few Presidents have been as enthusiastic about the nation or revealed the flaws in our government of majority rule such as

Trump. In the end, Trump's confidence didn't stop just before his demise. It promoted it. In the final months, the mission was managed by an amateur who drank a lot of money. Trump believed he could use his power to deflect a potentially dangerous illness. He shook off his army of pundits, hoping to enjoy the praise of his supporters. He was President only of his supporters and was a candidate to re-election without focusing on the middle. He did not even offer an idea of a strategy for the future term. He was a fierce fighter and flew to numerous mobilizations in Air Force One in the final stretch of the mission. He beat the notion of the most part thanks to a dazzling ground game, an innovative mission information program and an enthusiastic team of support.

However, ultimately the Trump administration concluded much like it began with a slight edge in the states necessary to isolate two of its rivals in the nation as well as Trump taking on America's evil forces over the better angels of heaven and flinging outrageous cases were rescinded.

Trump's administration was characterized by scandals and debates that changed as they were arousing. He didn't address the nation's racial ills' roots and instead rely by promoting a message of white protest. One of his most prominent political trends was the defection of white ladies, residents and school-instructed electors and free-moving members from the Republican Party.

The chances of re-appointment for him were uncovered in the course of the time a pandemic revealed his flaws in tandem with our own. The most notable among the mistakes was his insanity to handle an infection that put him in the hospital at the top of the mission. "On the off chance the President is never diagnosed with COVID, they win the choice of the president. Our research showed a significant fall when that happened particularly with rural schools, liberal, and men who are not liberal," says GOP planner Brad Todd. "Trump being a victim of COVID was a message to those in the group that his style of administration was a success in every way in his case and was not a realistic approach to alter."

The President's heritages are set within the context of crucial challenges. As COVID-19 struck, Trump pulled open the public's tears significantly more extensive. Just prior to Election Day, as the U.S. endured its most significant increase in the number of cases since the epidemic began, Trump ridiculed the infection as a source of intrigue for the media. "Counterfeit News Media is going completely out Covid" tweets Trump on October 27. "We are working on adjusting the direction of travel."

The electors were aware. In a stunning political year, over 235,000 Americans passed away and over 9 million of them were infected. The crisis required a president who was both testing and compassionate in advancing the best strategies to deal with the situation and mourn with American families that lost family members and friends in squalid room clinics.

Trump was defeated due to his "inability to communicate with the topic that citizens were most likely to think about and that was

Covid," says Sarah Longwell who was the founder of Republican Voters Against Trump (RVAT). While armies were deposed and shut down organizations, they avoided accepting their mature guardians and even taught their children, "what Trump did was chose to believe that Covid was not the most dominant aspect of people's daily lives,"" Longwell says. Trump's erroneous excuses could be causing deaths to seniors, a crucial segment of his alliance, which is especially susceptible to virus.

The enduring nature of the policies Trump has created for our government's popularity is unclear. The slits he created will be easy to repair. The vote in 2020 showed that there's still a large market for the sham-filled legislative issues he's promoting. And, perhaps most importantly, Trump won a large number of a greater quantity of votes than he did the previous four years. This was not the degraded rejection of his ideas and strategies that his opponents had envisioned. But, ultimately most of the American population chose to move forward.

One of the biggest flaws in Trump's offer to re-appoint him came nearly three years prior to the time he hired Brad Parscale as his mission chief. A computer-controlled administrator, Parscale ran an online media publicizing blitz on Facebook which helped Trump in winning the 2016 election. But, Parscale was likewise a political novice who was never faced with any kind of mission, not to mention one for a occupant President who had a very limited method of re-appointing. Parscale consumed lavishly, spending an enormous amount of money and also obtaining a significant cash advantage. When former New York City Mayor Michael Bloomberg paid for an Super Bowl advertisement to advance his short-lived official campaign The President's team offered $10 million to Trump's personal. "Brad has never been on any mission before," declares Mike DuHaime, a veteran Republican tactician and "to suddenly hold him on the hook for a billion dollar decision I think is inexplicably and a terrible decision." Parscale states that a number of others who were senior mission pioneers also backed the financial plan of the mission and his spending. "You might disagree in my process or my financial plan but saying that there was no plan was odd. This is a lie that's not true," Parscale, who was hesitant to respond to a request to provide input, read the clock for the seventh of November. "I experienced a distinct and modest spending, which was accepted by many people," Parscale says.

In July Trump was done and took over Parscale with appointee crusade director Bill Stepien. Insane and information-driven, Stepien began to control the financial plan of the mission and cutting T.V. spending as well as travel costs. However that, former Vice-President Joe Biden's huge money-making lead has hampered Trump's efforts to close the gap at the bottom.

The issue that was more troubling was the customer of Stephen. Trump has lost the well-known public vote by a staggering 3 million each year, but he did not attempt to reach out beyond his base of people who were savage to the bone. If all else is equal the president attempted to identify new voters--the majority of whom were not school-educated white males who were drawn to his insidious, often racist and incendiary manner. He was unable to win the well-known presidential vote by a far greater edge--the election is not running--as a result of an unforced series of mistakes that shattered his aid in what was later deemed to be conclusive states. Biden switched Michigan, Wisconsin, and Pennsylvania in three states that influenced Trump the presidency in the year 2016.

Trump lost Arizona after feuding with the state's favorite son, the late Republican Senator John McCain. Suppose he loses Georgia, which hadn't been called as of November seventh. In that case, it will be partly because of strong Democratic turnout around Atlanta, in the district formerly represented by the late Congressman John Lewis, whose civil-rights legacy Trump dismissed.

Amid a cross country uprising over fundamental prejudice, Trump denied the primary issues. He never endeavored to join the nation or address its shared agony. On June fifth, under about fourteen days after the killing of George Floyd, and with the country grasped by Black Lives Matter fights, Trump held a meandering aimlessly public interview to promote a factual positions report. "Ideally George is peering down the present moment and saying this is something incredible that is occurring for our nation," Trump said. "This is an extraordinary day for him. It's an extraordinary day for everyone." Polls indicated that most electors objected to Trump's treatment of the fights, and it cut into his help among white citizens who had lifted him to triumph last time.

By midsummer, when Americans had lived encircled, miserable lives for quite a long time, a considerable lot of the citizens who had upheld Trump in 2016 had soured on his initiative. "It's a 'wouldn't fret attitude, a woman in Ft. Lauderdale, Fla., said in a middle social occasion encouraged by RVAT in July, which TIME took note. "This is a period in a crisis. You ought to be with us. Moreover, I can't see it.

Toward the beginning of the year, the President's counsels considered his most grounded contention for re-appointment. When it cratered on the Covid, his mission attempted to paint him as the best individual to bring the economy back. With high joblessness and 12.6 million individuals unemployed by September, that may have been an unthinkable errand. The Covid finished the monetary sugar surge," says Timothy Naftali, a history specialist at New York University. That was his demise.

Regardless, Trump didn't adhere to the content. His end crusade contention was a reiteration of complaints against the media, against Dr. Anthony Fauci, against the ghost "misrepresentation" of remote democracy, against the hard truth of expanding COVID-19 case checks. He wouldn't recognize the inevitable in the last days of the vote check, perilously spreading unwarranted charges of wide-spread citizen extortion and unjustifiably guaranteeing that Democrats had attempted to "take" the political decision.

What citizens heard was an applicant centered around his issues, not theirs. "There's been an empathy deficiency issue with Donald Trump," says the student of history, Douglas Brinkley. It was a deficiency Trump demonstrated he was unable to fill.

As Election Day drew closer, Trump went to the vast government mechanical assembly he controls to save him, crossing a more significant amount of the lines for which he had been prosecuted in 2019.

He recruited government organizations as infantrymen in his mission, forcing the Food and Drug Administration and Centers for Disease Control and Prevention to adjust their COVID-19 suggestions in his work to make light of the pandemic. He inclined toward the Justice Department to help his partners and explore his political enemies. In July, his Postmaster General, Louis DeJoy, executed far-reaching developments that eased back conveyance similarly as a large number of electors were projecting voting forms via mail. Trump utilized government specialists to clear racial-equity dissenters from Lafayette Square in Washington, D.C., defy fights in Portland and convey to "Leftist run" urban areas to paint a picture of the disorder.

"Trump consistently needed to utilize our law-implementation experts such that he thought would be politically advantageous to him and particularly harming blue states and urban areas," says Miles Taylor, the previous head of staff at the Department of Homeland Security, the creator of an unknown 2018 New York Times commentary that blasted his administration.

These disappointments have made Trump the one thing he was raised to fear most: a washout. Right off the bat in his life, Trump went to the Manhattan church of Norman Vincent Peale, the evangelist who lectured self-acknowledgment and composed the 1952 top of the line book The Power of Positive Thinking. Be that as it may, in legislative issues, his ability was for directing outrage and disdain.

"Losing is rarely simple," Trump considered at his mission central command on Election Day. "Not for me, it's most certainly not." For a man who has desired commendation regardless of anything else, being the primary President in almost 30 years to be thrown away after a solitary term is a troublesome blow. His self-image might be wounded. Be that as it may, bearing its injuries, the nation is presently confronted with the test of how to recuperate.

Biden won in excess of 70 million votes, the second most noteworthy complete in American history. Broadly, he has a 47% portion of his vote and hopes to have won 24 states, including his cherished Florida and Texas.

He has an uncommon hold over huge wraps of this nation, an automatic association that has brought a close to a faction like dedication among many allies. After four years in the White House, his supporters considered his administration's fine print and clicked excitedly on the standing and conditions.

Any examination of his political shortcoming in 2020 additionally needs to recognize his political strength. Nonetheless, he was crushed, getting one of just four officeholders in the cutting-edge period not to get an additional four years. Likewise, he has become the primary President to lose the mainstream vote in sequential races.

Donald Trump won the administration in 2016 mostly because he was a standard busting political outcast who was set up to state what had recently been unsayable.

However, Donald Trump additionally lost the administration in 2020, mostly on the grounds that he was a standard busting political pariah. He was set up to state what had recently been unsayable.

Even though a significant part of the Trump base may well have decided in favor of him on the off chance that he had shot somebody on Fifth Avenue, his scandalous gloat from four years prior, other people who upheld him four years back were put off by his violent conduct.

This was particularly obvious in suburbia. Joe Biden enhanced Hillary Clinton's presentation in 373 rural provinces, encouraging him to pay back the Rust Belt conditions of Pennsylvania, Michigan, and Wisconsin, empowering him to pick up Georgia and Arizona. Donald Trump has a specific issue with rural ladies.

We saw again in the 2020 official political race what we had found in the 2018 mid-term political race - all the more exceptionally taught Republicans. Some of them had decided in favor of Trump four years prior, arranged to give him a possibility, though his administration was excessively undignified. Although they comprehended, he would be capricious, many found how he opposed such countless traditions and social standards off-putting and regularly hostile.

His forcefulness put them off. His stirring up of racial pressures. His utilization of bigoted language in tweets censuring minorities. His disappointment, on events, to satisfactorily censure racial oppression. His destroying of America's customary partners and his appreciation for dictator strongmen, for example, Vladimir Putin.

He unusual gloats about being "an entirely steady virtuoso" and such. His advancement of paranoid fears. His utilization of a most widely used language that occasionally made him sound more like a kingpin, for example, when he depicted his previous attorney Michael Cohen, who arrived at a supplication manage government investigators, as "a rodent."

At that point, there was what pundits criticized as his crawling tyranny, seen after the political race in his refusal to acknowledge the outcome.

During this mission, a telling second came in Pittsburgh when I visited with Chuck Howenstein on the stoop of his terraced home. A Trump ally in 2016, he decided in favor of Joe Biden.

"Individuals are worn out," he advised me. "They need to see regularity back in this nation. They need to see tolerability. They need to see this disdain stop. They need to see this nation joined together. Furthermore, that together will bring Joe Biden the administration."

A political issue for Trump was that he neglected to grow his help past his center Trump base. Nor did he make a decent attempt to do as such. In 2016, he won 30 states and frequently represented as though he was the President exclusively of a traditionalist, red America. The most intentionally troublesome leader of the previous 100 years, he made a little endeavor to charm blue America, the 20 expresses that decided in favor of Hillary Clinton.

Following four depleting years, numerous electors just needed an administration they could have on out of sight - a tenant of the White House who might act more traditionally. They had worn out on the childish ridiculing, the monstrous language, and the interminable showdown. They needed a re-visitation of some regularity.

Yet, the 2020 political race was not a re-run of the 2016 political decision. This time he was the occupant, not the guerilla. He had a safeguarding record, including his misusing of a Covid flare-up, which Election Day had killed above 230,000 Americans. In this time of negative partisanship, where governmental issues are frequently determined by detesting the resistance, he was not opposed to a scorn figure like Hillary Clinton.

Donald Trump was difficult to trash, which is incompletely why the Democratic foundation was so quick to have him as its official candidate. This 77-year-old anti-extremist took care of the work he was recruited to do, which was to paw back white average electors in the Rust Belt.

Was it in the quick result of his triumph in 2016, when individuals who had decided in favor of Trump mostly as a dissenting vote against the Washington political foundation right away had second thoughts? Large numbers of those citizens never anticipated that he should win.

Was it in the initial 24 hours of his administration, when he conveyed his "American Carnage" debut address - which depicted the nation as a close to the oppressed world of covered industrial facilities, given up specialists and abundance "tore" from working-class homes - before he yelled about the group size and pledged to keep utilizing Twitter? By dusk of his first entire day in control, it had become confident that Donald Trump would try to change the administration more than the administration transformed him.

Was it more combined, the snowball impact of such countless embarrassments, numerous such slurs, such a lot of staff turnover, thus much bedlam?

Or then again, was it because of the Covid, the most extraordinary emergency that overwhelmed his administration? Before the infection showed up on these shores, Trump's political essential signs were concrete. He had endured his indictment preliminary. His endorsement appraisals coordinated the most significant level it had been - 49%. He could flaunt a stable economy and the upside of incumbency: the twin factors that typically secure a sitting president a subsequent term. Regularly official decisions turn on a straightforward inquiry: is the nation good now than it was four years prior? After Covid hit and the monetary emergency that followed, it became practically challenging to present that defense.

In any case, it isn't right to state that the Covid destined the Trump administration.

Presidents frequently rise out of public seizures more grounded. Emergencies can regularly bring out the significance. That was valid for Franklin Delano Roosevelt, whose protecting of America from the Great Depression made him politically unassailable. George W Bush's underlying reaction to the assaults of September eleventh likewise supported his prevalence and caused him to win a subsequent term. So, it was in no way, shape, or form destined that Covid would complete Donald Trump. It was his messed-up treatment of the emergency that added to his fall.

Again, it merits recollecting that Donald Trump remained politically feasible up until the end, notwithstanding the nation encountering its most exceedingly terrible general wellbeing emergency over 100 years, its most significant financial crisis since the 1930s, and its most boundless racial disturbance since the last part of the 1960s.

Quite a bit of red America, and a very remarkable moderate development he came to overwhelm, will long for his return. He will keep on being the prevailing player in the medium development for quite a long time to come. Trumpism could wind up having a similar extraordinary impact on American traditionalism as Reaganism.

Joe Biden wins the administration.

Joe Biden has dominated the competition to turn into the following U.S. president, defeating Donald Trump following a precipice holder vote check after Tuesday's political race.

The BBC projects that Mr. Biden should win Pennsylvania's critical landmark, impelling him over the 270 constituent school vote edge needed to secure the White House.

The Trump lobby has demonstrated their up-and-comer doesn't plan to surrender.

The outcome makes Mr. Trump the first-term President since the 1990s.

The BBC's projection of Mr. Biden's triumph depends on the informal outcomes from states that have just wrapped up checking their votes and the expected results from states like Wisconsin, where the tally is proceeding.

The political decision has seen the highest turnout since 1900. Mr. Biden has won more than 73 million votes until now, the most ever for a U.S. official up-and-comer. Mr. Trump has drawn just about 70 million, the second-most elevated count ever.

President Trump had erroneously announced himself the champ of the political race when vote tallying was incomplete. He has since supposed inconsistencies in adding, yet has not introduced any proof of political decision extortion.

His mission has recorded a blast of claims in different states, and prior on Friday, as Mr. Biden showed up on the cusp of triumph, he stated: "This political decision isn't finished."

The political decision was battled as Covid cases, and passings kept on ascending across the United States. President Trump was contending a Biden administration would bring about lockdowns and monetary melancholy. Joe Biden blamed the President for neglecting to force adequate measures to control the spread of Covid-19.

Joe Biden is presently set to re-visitation of the White House, where he served for a very long time as President Barack Obama's appointee. At 78 years old, he will be the most seasoned President in American history, a record recently held by the man he has now conquered, Donald Trump, who is 74.

Joe Biden's extended triumph following four days of careful vote-tallying is the conclusion of an uncommon mission, led during an overwhelming pandemic and far and wide social distress, and against a generally unusual of officeholders.

In his third go after the administration, Mr. Biden figured out how to explore the political obstructions and guarantee success that, while maybe thin in the appointive school count, is projected to outperform Mr. Trump's general public complete by at any rate 4,000,000 votes.

With his projected triumph, Joe Biden becomes the most established man ever chosen for the White House. He carries with him the principal lady V.P., whose multi-ethnic legacy conveys with it various firsts.

Mr. Biden would now be able to start the challenging undertaking of arranging the progress to his new organization. He will have just shy of a quarter of a year to gather a bureau, decide strategy needs, and plan to oversee a country confronting various emergencies and forcefully isolated along sectarian lines.

Biden defeats Trump

I comprehend the mistake around evening time. I've lost myself multiple times. Be that as it may, presently, how nearly we give each other a possibility," Biden stated. "This is an excellent opportunity to mend in America."

California Sen. Kamala Harris, his running mate that will leave an imprint on the world as the key woman, the fundamental Black individual, and the essential individual of South Asian dive to become VP, saw the criticalness of her put on the stage Saturday night.

"While I may be the primary woman in this office, I won't be the last, considering the way that each and every youngster seeing around night time sees that this is a country of possible results," Harris said.

Prior in the day, the V.P. pick posted a video on Twitter of her triumph call beside Biden: "We did it, we did it, Joe. You will be going with the President of the United States.

Trump, who was on the green at CNN and various associations called the race for the past V.P., has exhibited no sign that he intends to give up. While in transit to his Virginia course, he tweeted: "I WON THIS ELECTION, BY A LOT!"

Notwithstanding, Biden partners - whose face covers reflected the great states of a pandemic-period political race filled the streets the country over in a depiction of treatment to laud the President-elect's victory.

Following four years of Trump's consistent lies, torturing, and defaming his political enemies, the past V.P. said he was racing to restore the nation's character and invest wholeheartedly back to the White House. Biden, who turns 78 close to the completion of this current month, will transform into the most settled President when he is presented in January amidst the most extremely dreadful general prosperity emergency in 100 years, the central monetary hang since the 1930s, and a public requital on fanaticism and police savagery that is so far unsure.

His political choice will end Trump's fierce hold tight Washington and decry the Republican, who has had a dependable obsession with winning, to the places of CEOs who lost after a lone term.

Past President Barack Obama conveyed a clarification that filled in as a recognition for his past V.P.'s character and mentioned that Americans set aside their political differences and give him a chance.

"Right when he walks around the White House in January, he'll face a movement of striking challenges no moving toward President really has - a fuming pandemic, a conflicting economy and value structure, a greater part controls framework in harm's way, and an air in peril," Obama created. "I understand he'll deal with the work with the possible advantages of every American on the most major level, whether or not he had their vote."

The past President mentioned that every American "give him a chance and credit him your assistance."

"The political choice outcomes at each level show that the country remains significantly and cruelly detached," Obama stated. "It will hold up to Joe and Kamala, yet all of us, to do our part - to interface past our typical scope of commonality, to check out others, to cut down the temperature and find some shared view from which to push ahead, us all of us that we are one nation, under God."

Biden's childhood province of Pennsylvania put him over the 270 constituent vote edge in an artistic bend and conveyed him to this White House. Biden had held a wide lead above Trump the nightfall of the political race. All things considered, as political race authorities checked a considerable number of early polling forms, the race moved drastically in support of Biden, rankling Trump and his partners. They knew the President's way to the White House was over without the province.

That the Keystone State was the last obstruction in Biden's manner to the White House was a fitting completion to a hard-struggled race given that the past V.P. has since a long time prior built up his image as "common Joe" from Scranton. In a visit that as of now seems, by all accounts, to be prophetic, he had made the last excursion to his childhood home in the city on Election Day ensuing to spending an enormous piece of the mission promising to put together the occupations of the many everyday residents whom Hillary Clinton lost to Trump in her 2016 offer.

On one of the family room dividers in the house where he grew up, he expressed: "From the House to the White House with the Grace of God," denoting his name and the date, "11.3.2020."

In this last day of the race, Biden's group tried harder to modify the Democrats' "blue divider" - and that ruse paid off with Biden winning Pennsylvania, Michigan, and Wisconsin, as indicated by CNN projections while holding Minnesota, which the President focused on in his re-appointment push.

Biden will likewise win Nevada, CNN projects, enlarging his Electoral College lead as polling forms keep being checked around the world. Georgia could make a beeline for a related, and votes were streaming in from Arizona, where Biden holds an edge.

Biden at present holds a 279-214 edge in the Electoral College.

As he watched his assumptions for re-arrangement being stifled with each tranche of votes in Pennsylvania, Trump lashed out on Twitter during the stressed vote check, trying to disrupt majority rule organizations with requests like "STOP THE COUNT."

The President dishonestly asserted the political race was being taken from him. The same number of early voting forms, which were frequently tallied after Election Day votes, arrived in his rival's section.

Confronting a profoundly energized nation, Biden had attempted to project comity and tolerance, and his longing to unite America.

"There won't be blue states and red kingdoms when we gain. Simply the United States of America," Biden announced Wednesday evening. "We are not foes. Whatever unites us as Americans is such a lot of more grounded than whatever can destroy us."

The triumph of Joseph Robinette Biden Jr., who fashioned a 50-year vocation as congressperson and V.P. from his Delaware property, is a round trip second that comes over 30 years after his first official mission.

Biden's life of misfortune - he covered his first spouse and his first girl, and his grown-up child Beau, who kicked the bucket in 2015, endure two mind aneurysms and remained in governmental issues after two bombed White House crusades - molded his picture as a man of strength and goodness. Those characteristics settled on him America's decision as a president who could bear a country's misery damaged by the deficiency of more than 234,000 residents to Covid-19, with millions jobless in a climate of severe economic vulnerability.

Biden's triumph implies that Trump's wrath filled administration - controlled by his patriotism, poisonous racial claims, ceaseless lying, and attack on just foundations - may come to be viewed as a chronicled variation as opposed to another type.

However, Biden faces a colossal assignment in joining the nation and tending to America's dissatisfaction with foundation figures like him, which prompted the current President's political ascent as an untouchable who was chosen on an influx of populism in 2016.

Biden is vowing to reestablish America's "spirit," which he says was undermined by Trump's disruptive methodology and cleanse the President's "America First" international strategy and revamp Washington's everyday situation of a worldwide initiative.

In any case, Democrats longing for "Another Deal" style time of change on medical services, the economy, environmental change, race, and perhaps, in any event, growing the Supreme Court will see their aspirations tempered by their absence of gains yet to be determined of intensity in Congress.

The Democrats will keep up control of the House of Representatives, CNN projected Saturday. However, Republicans fared much better than anticipated in many House races worldwide.

Inside a partitioned government, quite a bit of Biden's energy should be centered around ending a pandemic that is deteriorating. Wellbeing specialists at the University of Washington's Institute for Health Metrics and Evaluation project say the infection could guarantee almost 400,000 Americans lives when Biden is confirmed.

Joe Biden will be the following President of the United States. He won the political race on November third. Even though the final voting day occurred on November third, numerous Americans had cast a ballot early due to the COVID-19 pandemic. This implied that a considerable lot of the votes were included slower than in past races. It required some investment for anybody to realize who won. Regularly, it is discovered who won before the entirety of the votes are checked. At times it is recognized who won after a couple of states have capped a portion of their options.

After the votes were at long last tallied, it became realized that Joe Biden defeated President Donald Trump. Individuals have been angry at governmental issues in the U.S., which implied that more individuals cast a ballot than any other time in recent memory. More than 151 million individuals cast a vote in this political race. From the start, the race was a lot nearer than individuals suspected it would be, yet eventually, unmistakably, Joe Biden had won by a significant sum. The early polling forms made it look close at the outset.

Many individuals decided in favor of Trump than in 2016; in any case, it wasn't sufficient to beat Joe Biden.

Leftists are glad that Joe Biden won. Nonetheless, they are disturbed about how President Trump has responded to the misfortune. Trump would not surrender. On political race night, he lied and reported that he was the champ. Since the political decision, he has said that there was a misrepresentation in the political race and that many of these votes were illicit. Numerous individuals don't trust him, and there is no proof of extortion. Individuals don't have the foggiest idea whether Trump will take off from the White House all alone in January or if individuals should drive him out.

Previous VP Joe Biden has been chosen the 46th President of the United States. Biden's success has come after a hard-battled crusade during the tallness of the Covid pandemic. Biden's success is a notable triumph as he has gotten a more significant number of votes than any Presidential up-and-comer ever. The past record-holder was Barack Obama for his 2008 success. Biden's success is likewise critical for the way that occupant Presidents never lose decisions. Trump is the principal occupant President to lose a political decision in 28 years and merely the fourth officeholder to lose in the previous 100 years. In another memorable triumph, recently V.P. chooses Kamala Harris will be the principal lady V.P., the leading Black VP, and the primary Asian V.P. in the U.S.

We currently realize that Biden won a definitive triumph, yet because of the COVID-19 pandemic, the political decision results at first appeared to be close. A more significant number of Americans cast a ballot in the 2020 political race than in any political decision throughout the nation's entire existence. More than 30 million additional individuals cast a ballot in 2020, contrasted with 2016, even though the votes are tallied, and that number could increment. Because of the mind-boggling turnout, vote counters in numerous states were immersed with polling forms. More than 100 million individuals likewise chose to cast a ballot via mail, which isn't regular in the entirety of the U.S. Because of the diverse democratic and including rules in different states, the outcomes streamed in much more slowly this year than in earlier years.

Albeit the entirety of the votes never relies on political decision night, it is regular for the consequences of a political decision to be known on the night itself. This is done through projections dependent on the number of votes that have been checked, whose votes have been tallied, and the number of votes is remaining. For example, Associated Press has confounded calculations that calculate, report and anticipate each state's outcomes. When news associations are 99.5% sure of the work in a form, they will "call" the state for one applicant. This gives everybody an away from of who has won the political decision, now and again rapidly. In 1980, President Jimmy Carter surrendered to then-chosen one Ronald Reagan before the surveys had even shut on the west coast because the projections were so unequivocally in support of Reagan. It was evident before casting a ballot finished on the west coast that Reagan had won.

The current tenant of the White House keeps on projecting a resistant public stance, however. White House insiders, albeit flattened, have been imparting signs that Trump has no designs to yield until every battle is done. Five states are yet to report eventual outcomes.

For Biden, the present success covers an over multi-decade chase for the enormous prize. During that time, he has worried about the concern of numerous individual distresses in his twisting way to America's most noteworthy office.

Biden's triumph comes amid a most surprising territory for an official political decision. Across the nation, early voting forms did the star turn for Biden and his V.P. pick Kamala Harris in a political race changed by the Covid pandemic.

Biden's considerable advancement came around 9 am Friday EST when he broke into the lead in Pennsylvania and at first surpassed Trump by about 5,000 votes. From that point forward, that lead is just developing as votes keep on being tallied.

Strangely, this is where, in the prior week's final voting day, Trump advised citizens that he needed to "get the hellfire out of here." That was an indirect reference to the conditions constraining Trump to crusade in spots he won serenely in 2016; however, the paradox isn't lost regarding a Biden win here.

Biden is a sharp difference from Trump, both in the individual and political domain. The most recent three days specifically have demonstrated Americans look at that very distinction.

Biden went through consistently since November third attempting to ease pressures and conveying his messages with a minimal outward demonstration of uneasiness. The trained idea of the mission reaches out to plans for the intermediary period of the Trump administration. Two entire days before the eventual outcomes came, the Biden lobby uncovered its change site, underscoring its calm trust in what was to come.

"I request that everybody stay quiet. The cycle is working," Biden has said consistently. "It is the desire of the citizens. Nobody, not any other individual who picks the leader of the United States of America."

The Biden lobby trusts it has crossed the Pennsylvania challenge and is "blissful," as per correspondents on the ground in Delaware, the Biden base camp. He is at present driving by 30,000 votes there.

A great many votes are still to be tallied, yet even before we have the last count, Biden has virtually 73 million votes broadly, the most in American political history.

Trump is raging; he stays resistant and keeps charging "misrepresentation" in Pennsylvania and different milestones. His kids have tolled into the general White House emergency, in wording that by and large involve the broad curve between what's "legitimate" and "illicit."

Vote based up-and-comer Joe Biden has won the U.S. official political decision, primary U.S. media sources are anticipating.

CNN, NBC, and USA Today were among the sources that have extended success for the previous V.P. in Pennsylvania's landmark province. That would give Biden 273 Electoral College votes, getting him only past the 270 edges expected to win the political race.

The Associated Press fixes the current count at 290 for Biden and 214 for U.S. President Donald Trump.

Trump, notwithstanding, has not yielded and is probably not going to at any point shortly. In an assertion delivered not long after the projections of Biden's triumph, he stated: "We as a complex know why Joe Biden is racing to dishonestly act like the champ, and why his media partners are making a modest attempt to help him: they don't need reality to be uncovered. The basic reality is this political decision is a long way from being done." He proceeded to blame the Biden lobby for tallying unlawful polling forms and undermined lawful activity in the week ahead. His assertion is following clearing fear inspired notions the President advanced in a question and answered session on Thursday, without proof.

Trump's tweets were hailed on various occasions by Twitter Thursday for containing falsehood about the political decision. At a certain point, the President tweeted, "STOP THE COUNT!" in all covers.

"It's the ideal opportunity for America to join together. Also, to mend," Biden said in an assertion following the projections. "With the mission over, it's an ideal opportunity to put the indignation and the unforgiving manner of speaking behind us and meet up as a country." He is required to give a public location Saturday night.

Americans picked the following President in a political decision held during a furious Covid pandemic, with a considerable number of non-attendant voting forms overturning past timetables for vote tallying and results.

The President himself gotten the infection during the mission, reporting his determination on Twitter and going through a few days at Walter Reed Medical Center.

A bogus triumph guarantee by Trump early Wednesday; unmerited allegations of political decision extortion; case, including claims tossed out by decided in Michigan and Georgia; and encounters at vote including areas in Detroit and Phoenix loaned a demeanor of flimsiness to the nation's center vote based cycle this week.

The financial exchange this week revitalized on the rising possibilities for a Democrat-drove White House and Republican-drove Senate. The subsequent gridlock would slow down clearing Democratic changes, specifically a possible expansion in duties and guidelines.

The three crucial U.S. files recorded their most significant seven day stretch of exchanging since April. The Dow Jones Industrial Average chose up 6.87% during the week, opening with 26,787.65 and shutting down at 28,323.40. The NASDAQ Composite Index began the week at 11,001.70 and shut it at 11,895.23, developing by 9 01%. The S&P 500 picked up 7.32% throughout the week, shutting down at 3,509.44.

The Incoming Biden-Harris Administration: Biden, 77, filled in as a U.S. congressperson from Delaware from 1973 to 2009 preceding turning out to be V.P. under President Barack Obama two terms.

In 2017, Obama gave Biden the Presidential Medal of Freedom.

Kamala Harris, 56, will be the primary female and the principal African American to hold V.P.'s workplace in U.S. history. Harris filled in as California's chief legal officer before her political race to the U.S. Senate in 2016.

The thing that's inevitably coming For Biden: The direst need confronting the Biden organization is undoubtedly the Covid, a pandemic minimized by Trump that is flooding broadly in the second influx of contaminations and that has prompted significant financial constriction and occupation misfortunes.

The U.S. hit more than 120,000 day by day cases unexpectedly on Thursday and afterward hit almost 130,000 on Friday, as per Reuters.

Biden is getting back to a White House shaken by the outrages of a reprimanded president whose relatives have been interlaced with his authority obligations and who has made verbally abusing and day by day articulating of falsehoods signs of his administration.

On the world stage, Trump has frequently demonstrated warmth toward strongmen, for example, Russia's Vladimir Putin, turning the post-World War II international strategy of the U.S. topsy turvy.

Trump was arraigned toward the end of last year by the House of Representatives on articles of maltreatment of intensity and block of Congress, blamed for meddling with a House examination of Trump's solicitation to the Ukrainian President to research Biden and his child Hunter.

It takes 270 electors to become the next President of the United States. This afternoon, Biden broke that barrier by winning in Pennsylvania, which is worth 20 electors. He was thus elected the 46th president of the United States.

Since then, Biden has also won Nevada's six electoral votes. In total, according to A.P., the Democrat now stands at 290 electors, while Trump has 214. No winner has yet been announced in three states, but it no longer matters for the result.

Conclusion

The time came on November 3, 2020. With the election of a new president, it will finally be clear which way the U.S. will go in the next four years. Or is it not? Sure, Joe Biden is currently well ahead in all surveys, but what does that mean? Democrats are concerned about two things.

On the one hand, the specter of the U.S. election in 2016 also hangs over this year's polls. Because even then, based on the polls, a victory for Hillary Clinton was a foregone conclusion. But even assuming that things will turn out more positively this time around, there is still a second factor. Because the fact is that nobody knows how Donald Trump will behave on election night.

Donald Trump may not admit defeat to Joe Biden.

That could be problematic, especially if the result between Donald Trump and Joe

Biden should be close. Then the otherwise normal transition from one presidency to another could go entirely out of joint. The courts, the Congress, and even the military might have to decide on the country's weal and woe in extreme cases.

The U.S. Constitution treats this question rather negligently. Indeed, it is precisely regulated when the term of office of a president ends and when that of the successor begins, namely on January 20 at noon. But what happens if someone does not remain by the unwritten laws stays completely open. After an election, the change in power is ultimately based on the fact that those involved are ready to officially admit their defeat. But Donald Trump is far from that.

Donald Trump spoke of fraud in the 2016 U.S. election.

That is entirely in his nature because Donald Trump is not known as a good loser. Even after he won the U.S. election in 2016 *, he insisted that not everything had gone entirely - otherwise, he kept stiffly and firmly, Hillary Clinton would hardly have received almost three million more votes than him. So when he won, he questioned the legitimacy of the election. So it would be nonsensical to assume that Donald Trump would accept a defeat in the 2020 U.S. election.

In addition to obtaining the Electoral College in a landslide, I won the popular vote if you deduct the millions from people who voted illegally.

www.ingramcontent.com/pod-product-compliance
Lightning Source LLC
Chambersburg PA
CBHW050402120526
44590CB00015B/1796